More Political Babble

The Dumbest Things
Politicians Ever Said

DAVID OLIVE

Illustrated by Barry Blitt

John Wiley & Sons, Inc.

New York ♦ Chichester ♦ Brisbane ♦ Toronto ♦ Singapore

To Adrian, boy wonder

ISBN 1620457075

Printed in the United States of America

10 9 8 7 6 5 4 3 2 1

The world is weary of statesmen whom democracy has degraded into politicians.

BENJAMIN DISRAELI

Contents

Preface

Politics is always in season, but never more so than in the run-up to a presidential election. This is when boastful and apocalyptic rhetoric floods the airwaves, and when coffee shop talk and the deliberations of earnest editorial writers alike turn on the hyperbole and hypocrisy of candidates whose shortcomings, real and perceived, are assessed with an even greater sense of urgency than usual.

This book is intended as a tour of all the important campaign stops, and of what happens between campaigns besides.

Thomas Jefferson said, "Whenever a man has cast a longing eye on offices, a rottenness begins in his conduct." His assessment, if broadened to include "inanity" along with rottenness, is borne out in Chapter 1, "On the Campaign Trail," where Texas gubernatorial candidate George W. Bush invites voters to "Read my ears"—echoing his father's "Read my lips, no new taxes" pledge; Virginia senator Charles Robb accuses his opponent Oliver North of being in bed with the Ayatollah; and obscure presidential candidate Lamar Alexander hopes someday to be as famous as Kato Kaelin, star witness in the O.J. Simpson trial.

In Chapter 2, "The Domestic Front," a president fond of naps, Calvin Coolidge, rouses himself periodically to ask, "Is the country still here?" Ronald Reagan asserts that you can tell a lot about a man by the color of jelly beans he eats. California governor Pete Wilson threatens, good-naturedly, to kneecap anyone who doesn't like what he has to say. North Carolina senator Jesse Helms threatens to sing Dixie to the first African-American member of the United States Senate. And Senator Howell Heflin of Alabama vows never again to accidentally bring his wife's panties to the office in place of a handkerchief.

At center stage, meanwhile, the political superstars of the day vie for attention. Bill Clinton brushes up on his hog-calling skills, faults himself for being an "Eisenhower Republican," insists that McDonald's fare isn't necessarily junk food, and confesses that "I made my lowest grade in conduct, because I talked too much in school and the teachers were always telling me to stop." His humble sidekick, Al Gore, insists that the proper title for addressing the vice president is "Your Adequacy," but complains when Congressman Joe Kennedy attracts more admirers than he does at a public event, calling out, "Hey lady, what about me?"

If Bill Clinton, fighting his problem with the "stature gap," knows that "I've got to be more like John Wayne" and prays for divine intervention at every opportunity, Bob Dole knows that *he* is utterly capable of governing. He's certain of his qualifications to be president because, as he says, "There has never been a president named Bob," and the time for that has surely arrived. In contrast to the rumored spats between Bill and Hillary, Dole says, "I don't think I'm mean. . . . I don't throw things at my wife or the staff." He worries about the fate of the nation in the hands of his rivals, observing about publicity hound Phil Gramm, for instance, that "everybody says the most dangerous place in the Capitol is between Phil and a TV camera." Dole despairs that so many candidates for office trade on their supposed lives of youthful deprivation: "I listen to all these politicians. They were all born in a log cabin. Give me a break."

Newt Gingrich's sense of self-importance also is beyond measurable limits, and is even more baldly stated. "I have an enormous personal ambition," he has admitted. "I want to shift the entire planet. And I'm doing it. . . . I represent real power." Gingrich believes "people like me are what stand between us and Auschwitz" and that overthrowing the Democrats in Congress was a great victory for the nation because Democrats "get up every morning knowing that to survive they need to do only two things: They lie regularly and they cheat." Newt is a futurist who anticipates the day when "people aboard space shuttles—the DC-3s of the future—will fly out to the Hiltons and Marriotts of the solar system"; and he's a pragmatist who understands that "victory is the avoidance of being crushed." He can't help it if his critics are "fixated and pathologically disoriented." Gingrich does fret, though, that if he doesn't start exercising soon, he will be starring in a movie called *The Last Couch Potato*.

A man of remarkably numerous contradictions, even by the standards of modern public life, Gingrich is both "a moderate" and "essentially a revolutionary"; "not a strong believer in religion" and a man who has "a vision of an America in which a belief in the Creator is once again at the center of defining being an American"; a man who feels that "Democrats are the enemy of normal Americans" and also insists that "every Republican has much to learn from studying what Democrats did right"—notably the New Deal and racial integration.

Political life is full of things "Better Left Unsaid" (Chapter 11), "Invective and Ridicule" (Chapter 12), and "Explications" (Chapter 15), all of which reveal the true beliefs of political figures—and the political process—more fully than any press release or stump speech. Media Relations (Chapter 13) also bear out the essential love-hate relationship between politicians and the people. "Avoid this crowd like the plague," Barbara Bush, pointing at a group of reporters, wisely counseled Hillary Clinton. In a faux angry moment, Al Gore unbraided David Letterman for his frequent Clinton put-downs: "That's the president of the United States you're talking about, pinhead." Uncharitable impressions are in no short supply on the other side as well. "He reminds every American woman of her first husband," columnist Art Buchwald said of George Bush. "He ate everything but the drapes," an astonished Tom Brokaw reported after a Bill Clinton luncheon at the White House with television news anchors. "He's a man who does like to put it down." President Clinton, it seems, is able to win the media's respect for only a few moments at a time. "He's turned the corner, mastered the job, bridged the stature gap," *Newsweek* said of Clinton's work in securing passage of the North American Free Trade Agreement. "Until next week."

Happily, humor sometimes intrudes on the harsh machinations of political life. "Unlike the president," New Jersey governor Christine Todd Whitman said of her experiences with marijuana, "I inhaled. And then I threw up." An Indiana newspaper editor greets reports of a new Dan Quayle visitor center in his town by concluding, "I suppose it would be a little more interesting than an Ed McMahon museum." Bill Clinton favors a jogging T-shirt that reads, "Why yes, I am a rocket scientist," and an admiring Gingrich allows that Clinton would make a good frat president, somebody who'd be fun to have a beer with.

As the trumpets once again sound, calling fearless candidates to the arena to strut before a skeptical audience of voters, we're reminded of La Rochefoucauld's observation: "It is easier to appear worthy of a position one does not hold, than of the office which one fills." On that basis, one supposes, we should be charitable as we watch the show, thankful that our own character and track records are not on trial. Still, it's fair to wonder, after contemplating the bizarre comments to which political leaders are so often given, if Thomas More was on to something good when he set down a law in his *Utopia* that stipulated, "Anyone who deliberately tries to get himself elected to a public office is permanently disqualified from holding one."

For all their failings, our leaders probably deserve our sympathy, if not always our respect. On close inspection, we find some talented leaders among the mere attention-seekers and time-servers. The advice that freshman congressman Harry Truman received is as sobering today as it was when first offered in 1934. "Harry, don't start out with an inferiority complex," Truman was told by a fellow congressman. "For the first six months you'll wonder how the hell you got here, and after that you'll wonder how the hell the rest of us got here."

And we'll wonder why we voted to put them there. It must have something to do with our faith in the democratic process, which, judging from the alternatives, isn't *entirely* misplaced.

Acknowledgments

I wish to thank the staff of John Wiley & Sons, and in particular my editor, P. J. Dempsey, for their assistance in making this book possible. As inspirations I cite, and heartily recommend as delightful reading, William Manchester's *The Glory and the Dream: A Narrative History of America, 1932–1972* (Bantam Books, 1980); Paul F. Boller, Jr.'s, *Presidential Anecdotes* (Penguin Books, 1982); Paul Slansky's *The Clothes Have No Emperor: A Chronicle of the American 80s* (Simon & Schuster, 1989); Peggy Noonan's *What I Saw At The Revolution: A Political Life in the Reagan Era* (Ballantine Books, 1990); and Richard Ben Cramer's *What It Takes: The Way to the White House* (Random House, 1992).

◆ 1 ◆

On the Campaign Trail

Whenever a man has cast a longing eye on offices, a rottenness begins in his conduct.

THOMAS JEFFERSON

If you would know the depth of meanness of human nature, you have got to be a prime minister running a general election.

Canadian prime minister JOHN A. MACDONALD

God ordained that I should be the next president of the United States.

President WOODROW WILSON, *disabusing Democratic National Committee chairman William McCombs of any notion that he or the party deserved any credit for Wilson's victory at the polls*

I think the American public wants a solemn ass as president and I think I'll go along with them.

CALVIN COOLIDGE

America's future is still ahead of us.

> New York governor THOMAS E. DEWEY, *campaigning for the presidency in 1948, bowing to cautious advisers who counseled him not to say anything controversial. Other Deweyisms, a collection of which was made available for the press's amusement by the Truman campaign, include: "Ours is a magnificent land. Every part of it"; "The miners in our country are vital to our welfare"; "Everybody that rides in a car or bus uses gasoline and oil"; "Our streams abound with fish."*

—————— Reality Check ——————

Isn't it harder in politics to defeat a fool, say, than an abler man?

> THOMAS E. DEWEY *in 1948, commenting to aides during his unsuccessful campaign to replace Harry Truman as president*

———————— ♦ ————————

[They] want two families in every garage.

> HARRY TRUMAN, *campaigning for reelection in 1948, on the Republicans*

Ben Hogan for President. If We're Going to Have a Golfer For President, Let's Have a Good One.

> *Bumper sticker that appeared during the Eisenhower administration, criticizing the president for spending too much time on the links*

Do you understand? I want to get from there [pointing to his allotted backbench seat] to there [Prime Minister Lester Pearson's seat] pretty quick.

> JEAN CHRÉTIEN *at age 29, a few days after first being elected a*
> *member of the Canadian Parliament, after the seating plan was*
> *explained to him. Chrétien achieved his goal in 1993, 30 years later,*
> *at age 59.*

Throw the rascals in.

> *Campaign slogan of* NORMAN MAILER *when he and running mate*
> *Jimmy Breslin sought the New York mayoralty in 1969*

──────── **Reality Check** ────────

Show me a good loser, and I'll show you a loser.

> JIMMY CARTER *in prepresidential days, unapologetic*
> *about his raw ambition to be a winner in politics*

──────────── ♦ ────────────

Well, I've got a big family, and lots of friends.

> GEORGE BUSH *in 1978, when asked why he would make a*
> *good president*

Introducing John Buchanan to this group is like introducing a dog to a fire hydrant.

> CLARA JEFFERSON, *head of a Tory women's group, introducing Tory*
> *premier John Buchanan of Nova Scotia at a party function in*
> *the 1980s*

It is easier to appear worthy of a position one does not
hold, than of the office which one fills.

LA ROCHEFOUCAULD

─────────── ♦ ───────────

The nation is in crying need of your moral vision!
Vice President and presidential candidate GEORGE BUSH *in 1987,*
praising Jerry Falwell in a bid to secure the Christian Fundamentalist
vote

He can stand eye-to-eye—with my daughter.
Representative RICHARD GEPHARDT *(D–Mo.) in 1987, planning the*
podium arrangements for a debate with Michael Dukakis, his
diminutive rival for the Democratic presidential nomination

The only thing I know I'm running for, as of this day, is the kingdom
of heaven.

Senator JESSE HELMS *(R–N.C.)*

Vote for the Crook. It's Important.
Bumper sticker sported by supporters of Governor Edwin Edwards
(D–La.) during his 1991 race against white supremacist David Duke.
Edwards, who won the election, had endured a series of ethics-related
investigations of his conduct in office.

Wennlund has an obscure, undistinguished record, and he's a poor dresser, too.

> RAY HANANIA, *candidate for the Illinois state assembly, in 1992, on incumbent Larry Wennlund, whom he challenged to a three-round boxing match*

Well, now we've got the conservative crap out of the way.

> TORIE CLARKE, *a spokesperson for the Bush campaign, in 1992, after the speeches of Ronald Reagan and Patrick Buchanan at the Republican National Convention*

Did he speak in complete sentences?

> *Senator* AL GORE (*D–Tenn.*), *vice-presidential candidate, in 1992, on George Bush's attack on Bill Clinton's health-care plan*

———————— **Reality Check** ————————

I don't dare ask how many hundreds of George Bush cards you have to trade to get one Michael Jordan.

> *President* GEORGE BUSH *in 1992, on a new set of presidential trading cards*

———————— ◆ ————————

Well, whose else's—who else's—could it be?

> GEORGE BUSH *in 1992, saying abortion is ultimately a woman's own decision. Bush was understood to be opposed to abortion.*

I've referred occasionally to my opponent—"the other guy" and even "the governor of a certain state with a profitable chicken industry on the Mississippi River located somewhere between Texas and Oklahoma."

> GEORGE BUSH, *campaigning for reelection in 1992, on Bill Clinton, whom he rarely mentioned by name. There are no states between Texas and Oklahoma.*

What the heck [is Bill Clinton] talking about when he describes a President's—quote—here's what he called it: "A President's powerless moments when countries are invaded, friends are threatened, Americans are held hostage, and our nation's interests are on the line." . . . Well, let me say, Governor Clinton: If America is powerless when our nation's interests are on the line, who else do you suppose is going to take care of us? My America is not powerless.

> GEORGE BUSH, *campaigning for reelection in September 1992. In the August speech to which Bush referred, Clinton spoke of "perilous," not "powerless" moments.*

I'll put this as delicately as I possibly can: Fecal coliform bacteria.

> GEORGE BUSH *in 1992, citing one of the environmental problems in Bill Clinton's Arkansas*

I don't want to run the risk of ruining what is a lovely recession.

> GEORGE BUSH *in 1992, during a campaign stop in Ridgewood, New Jersey. He meant to say "reception."*

I'm just waiting for one of you to come up with a robot that can give a public speech. I'm sure it will make my life easier and also yours.

> GEORGE BUSH *in 1992, to scientists at the Sandia National Laboratories in Albuquerque, New Mexico*

Would you please shut up and sit down!

> GEORGE BUSH *in 1992, to a group of POW–MIA families protesting a campaign speech in Crystal City, Virginia*

Sit down and shut up.

> BILL CLINTON *in 1992, to a heckler in Chicago yelling at him about adultery*

Actually, I'm a little envious of Murphy Brown. At least she's guaranteed of coming back this fall.

> DAN QUAYLE *in 1992, in an aside to Candice Bergen, the actress who played the TV sitcom character Murphy Brown, during a campaign speech*

We raised taxes on the American people and put this country right into recession.

> DAN QUAYLE *in 1992, inadvertently apologizing for President Bush's broken "no new taxes" pledge in a renewed call for tax relief*

We will be asking them to join with us. I'm also going to ask them to help us to change the Congress. It's not just enough to change the president if we want to change America.

> DAN QUAYLE *in 1992, wooing Ross Perot supporters and appearing to endorse the removal of his boss from the White House*

Here's the kitchen. Here's the hallway. We've got plenty of closet space. Look—no skeletons.

> RUSS FEINGOLD, *successful 1992 candidate for a Senate seat from Wisconsin, during a TV ad in which he gave viewers a tour of his home*

I think it's about time we voted for senators with breasts. After all, we've been voting for boobs long enough.

> *Arizona senatorial candidate* CLAIRE SARGENT *in 1992, on women candidates. Sargent was not elected.*

We believe he wanted to win in the worst way.

> DON ESLINGER, *sheriff of Seminole County, Florida, in 1992, after state representative candidate Eric Kaplan allegedly shot at the home of his opponent, Representative Bob Starks, whose wife was wounded in the assault*

Students don't vote. Do you expect me to come in here and kiss your ass?

> *Senator* WYCHE FOWLER (R–Ga.) *in 1992, to young volunteers campaigning for deficit reductions. Fowler denied making the comment; the volunteers insisted he did.*

But that I'm out of touch with the American people, that I don't know people are hurting, I know it. I feel it. We pray about it, and I mean that literally at night, and, uh, many things, the various, where I don't care about, don't know about education or don't, I mean, we've got a sound approach, innovative, revolutionary approach, and so I have to make that clear.

GEORGE BUSH *in 1992*

I'll put you down as a doubtful, fella.

GEORGE BUSH *in 1992, to a caller on Larry King's talk show, who said, "I think you're out of touch. I am not happy with you."*

─────────── **Reality Check** ───────────

You will reach a point where you can only be sure of two votes—yours and your wife's.

Former president JIMMY CARTER'*s advice to Richard Gephardt, candidate for the Democratic presidential nomination, in 1988, on the inevitable low points in every political campaign*

───────────── ♦ ─────────────

Don't ask me. I'm not a numbers guy. I don't know anything about economics.

A 25-year-old Bloc Québécois candidate in the 1993 Canadian federal election, when pressed for details on the BQ's economic policy

I look at my agenda for "le hanky panky" and it's not there.
>KIM CAMPBELL *in 1993, bemoaning the lack of time for a private life*

Do you have something for my mouth, too?
>A gaffe-prone KIM CAMPBELL *in 1993, gamely accepting from a Montreal radio talk-show host a pair of earplugs for blocking out criticism*

You know, if we all go, Manning will be prime minister.
>*Liberal leader* JEAN CHRÉTIEN, *referring to Reform Party leader Preston Manning, in a chat with reporters moments after his campaign plane made a bumpy landing following an announcement from the pilot that the brakes were malfunctioning*

——— Reality Check ———

Let me win the election and after that you come and ask me questions about how I run a government.
>*Liberal leader* JEAN CHRÉTIEN *in 1993, dismissing reporters who sought details on how he would preserve social programs in times of severe deficit constraints*

———— ♦ ————

Orange says friendliness, brown dependability, red assertiveness.
>*Advice on clothing selections in a 1993 Liberal Party of Canada guidebook for female candidates, who tripled their seat count in the House of Commons in 1993 to 36*

Don't compare me to the Almighty, compare me to the alternative.

Ontario premier BOB RAE *in 1993, on the proper criteria for assessing his performance*

I am running for governor not because I am George and Barbara's son. I am running because I am George P. and Noelle and Jeb's father.

JEB BUSH *in 1993, kicking off his bid for governor of Florida. Over in Texas, meanwhile, gubernatorial candidate George W. Bush said: "I am not running for governor because I am George Bush's son. I am running because I am Jenna and Barbara's father."*

The bottom line is there have been a lot of nuts elected to the United States Senate.

Senator CHARLES GRASSLEY *in 1994, on why Republicans shouldn't oppose Virginia GOP senate nominee Oliver North*

—————— **Reality Check** ——————

Anyone who deliberately tries to get himself elected to a public office is permanently disqualified from holding one.

THOMAS MORE *in* Utopia

————————— ♦ —————————

[The Liberals] are a beanbag kind of party that looks like the last person who sat in it.

BOB RAE, *leader of the Ontario New Democratic Party*

Read my ears.

> George W. Bush, *during his successful 1994 gubernatorial campaign in Texas, mimicking his father's infamous 1988 "Read my lips, no new taxes" pledge*

To be perfectly blunt, I'm much more intelligent.

> Dawn Clark Netsch, *Democrat candidate for governor of Illinois, in 1994, on why she's better qualified for the job than incumbent Jim Edgar, who won reelection*

I can understand that if you have sold arms to the Ayatollah why you might not be quite as sensitive to the need to get assault weapons off our streets.

> *Senator* Charles Robb (D–Va.) *in a desperate and ultimately successful 1994 effort to stave off defeat at the hands of challenger Oliver North*

Well, there is going to be a need for inspiration too. We are going to have to explain how balanced-budget amendments and orphanages, and doing away with school lunch programs and racial preferences—how all that adds up to hope.

> Lamar Alexander *in 1995, attempting to soften the negative tone set by himself and other contenders for the GOP presidential nomination*

I am encouraged by the example of Kato Kaelin, who was relatively unknown until two weeks ago.

LAMAR ALEXANDER in 1995, on his chances in the race for the 1996 GOP presidential nomination. Kaelin, a friend of O.J. Simpson, had just given controversial testimony in the Simpson double-murder trial.

We've put an end to the Argentina of decadence and paralysis. People aren't stupid and don't want to return to the past. Either it's me or chaos.

CARLOS MENEM, during his successful 1995 campaign for reelection as president of Argentina

——————— **Reality Check** ———————

There are probably a couple hundred thousand people who could do a better job.

Senator PHIL GRAMM (R–Tex.) in 1995, on what kind of president he would make

——————————— ◆ ———————————

I will no longer show off my rump.

SUSY DIAZ, victorious as a candidate in Peru's 1995 congressional elections, swearing off her previous vocation as an exotic dancer

I can think of 675 million good reasons not to run against John Kerry.

MITT ROMNEY, 1994 GOP senate candidate in Massachusetts, in 1995, on the recent marriage of Massachusetts Senator John Kerry and heiress Teresa Heinz, who is said to be worth $675 million

• 2 •

The Domestic Front

Yes, they cannot say now that I am a president without a party!
President JOHN TYLER, *whose response on hearing that his wife had been publicly taunted by critics who said her husband was a man without a party was to give a large party in the usually somber Tyler White House*

How could I? I know only two tunes. One of them is Yankee Doodle and the other isn't.
President ULYSSES GRANT, *when asked at a concert if he had enjoyed the music*

My father used to say that it was wicked to go fishing on Sunday. But he never said anything about draw-poker.
President GROVER CLEVELAND

Yes—the right and the wrong.

> President WOODROW WILSON, *on being asked to*
> *consider that there are two sides to every question*

———————————— ◆ ————————————

He certainly is a wonder, and I wish we could make him president of the United States. There couldn't be a better one.

> FRANKLIN ROOSEVELT *at the conclusion of World War I, on Herbert*
> *Hoover, who was widely acclaimed for his efficiency as director of*
> *European relief at the end of the war*

I thought I could swing it.

> CALVIN COOLIDGE, *when asked what his first thought was on*
> *learning that he was to assume the presidency following the*
> *assassination of President Warren Harding*

Is the country still here?

> President CALVIN COOLIDGE, *waking from one of his customary*
> *White House naps, which lasted from two to four hours*
> *each afternoon*

Well, don't you think they ought to be represented too?

> President CALVIN COOLIDGE, *when an associate objected to the*
> *proposed appointment of an industrialist to a public office, saying,*
> *"But, Mr. President, that fellow's a son of a bitch"*

The only thing that really surprised us when we got into office was that things were just as bad as we had been saying they were; otherwise we have been enjoying it very much.

President JOHN KENNEDY, *when asked at the conclusion of his first year as president if he was happy in the job*

In your sunset years, you will tell your children and grandchildren how life in America used to be when men were free.

RONALD REAGAN *in 1962, campaigning against the evils of socialized medicine as represented by the Kerr-Mills and Anderson-King bills, forerunners to Medicaid and Medicare, respectively*

I am now at my full height, which is not very imposing. Fortunately, these are houses of debate where the measurement is from the shoulders up, rather than the shoulders down.

TOMMY DOUGLAS, *leader of Canada's New Democratic Party, in 1962, on being told that when speaking in the Commons he must stand up*

The single most dangerous piece of legislation ever introduced in the Congress.

Senator JESSE HELMS, *on the Civil Rights Act of 1964*

There would be untold incidents of betrayal committed by these weak, morally sick wretches who had sought and obtained government employment.

Senator JESSE HELMS *in 1964, describing homosexuals as a risk to national security*

Son, they are all my helicopters.
> President LYNDON JOHNSON, *after a Marine officer gave him directions, saying, "That's your helicopter over there, sir."*

I'm very existential.
> Senator GARY HART *in the mid-1980s, on his reputation as a man with too many ideas and too little practical experience as a lawmaker. On first meeting the new Soviet leader Mikhail Gorbachev, Hart attempted a quick introduction of himself and was interrupted: "I know about you," said Gorbachev. "They call me the Soviet Gary Hart. They say I have New Ideas."*

—————— **Reality Check** ——————

Edmonton isn't exactly the end of the world, but you can see it from there.
> *Calgary mayor* RALPH KLEIN, *on the rivalry between Alberta's two largest cities*

———————— ♦ ————————

You can tell a lot about a fella's character by whether he picks out all of one color or just grabs a handful.
> President RONALD REAGAN, *explaining to an aide why he liked to have a jar of jelly beans on hand for important meetings. Some 40 million jelly beans were consumed at Reagan's inaugural galas in 1981.*

I'm the one with the watch.

President RONALD REAGAN, *on the scene in the 1951 film* Bedtime for Bonzo *that finds actor Reagan in bed with chimpanzee Bonzo*

Thanks very much for sending me the clipping. . . . I have never felt so young and virile.

> *President* RONALD REAGAN, *in reply to a letter from a citizen who cited a newspaper account of a speech by a California state senator who favored prescribing birth-control devices for teenage girls without parental consent, claiming that "illegitimate births to teenaged mothers have increased alarmingly while Reagan has been in office"*

Don't get sick.

> *Slogan that Democrats applied to George Bush's modest health-care reform proposals*

I asked for an ambassadorship to a small country with a warm climate, no army . . . and where all they do is have cocktail parties.

> *Arkansas state representative* LLOYD GEORGE *in 1992, after welcoming President-elect Bill Clinton to Little Rock*

In the words of George Bernard Shaw . . . "Two roads diverged in a wood, and I—I took the one less traveled by."

> *Indiana governor* EVAN BAYH *in 1992, calling for educational excellence at a meeting of the Education Commission of the States. The poem quoted is by Robert Frost.*

I'm the most formidable figure on the court because I own the league. They all work for me and I am notoriously ungrateful to people who make me look bad.

> MARIO CUOMO *in 1993, on his influence with players in his staff basketball games*

All that hair, all those teeth—you gotta run scared.
Massachusetts governor WILLIAM WELD *in 1993, on*
speculation that he would be challenged for his job by
Representative Joe Kennedy in the next election

———————————— ◆ ————————————

I think Dan Quayle—I don't expect any of you to agree with this—I think he's got the best political mind in the White House.
Governor WILLIAM WELD *in 1992, on the vice president. Responding*
to the remark, White House political director Ronald Kaufman said,
"Are you kidding me?"

If the majority of the public only knew that bills are frequently passed in the wee hours of the morning, not having been read by the majority, some of whom are too drunk to read them at that stage even if they wanted to, we would all be thrown out of office.
Former Manitoba Liberal Party leader SHARON CARSTAIRS *in her*
1993 memoirs

Experience in what? Making a jackass of yourself in Question Period?
Reform Party of Canada leader PRESTON MANNING *the day after his*
party won 52 seats in the 1993 election, on the alleged lack of
governing experience of his newly elected caucus colleagues. Question
Period is the 45-minute parliamentary session in which the government
responds to questions—and heckling—from fellow parliamentarians.

If you ask questions, you start to think what could make it better and that's when you start thinking negatively.

Canadian prime minister JEAN CHRÉTIEN's *argument in 1994 against needless debate over the need to change perceived ills of the status quo, which only raises hopes that can't be fulfilled*

You made me feel young again.

Governor MARIO CUOMO *of New York in 1994, to a businesswoman who told him she "imagined him naked" whenever she needed to calm herself*

I didn't bet him anything. New York doesn't have anything I want.

Governor ANN RICHARDS *of Texas in 1994, on receiving a bouquet of yellow roses from New York governor Cuomo after the Dallas Cowboys defeated the Buffalo Bills in the Super Bowl*

You don't want to look like you're trying to Velcro yourself to the president.

MACK MCLARTY, *former White House chief of staff, in 1994, on why he took a West Wing basement office instead of trying to retain one closer to the Oval Office*

I wouldn't say prayer, because then you ask what prayer. I don't think there is any problem with a moment of silence. It's when most kids get to think of whether they remembered their shoes for the sixth-period gym class.

CHRISTINE TODD WHITMAN, *Republican governor of New Jersey, in 1995, expressing less-than-zealous endorsement of calls by many GOP leaders for school prayer*

I feel there should be a recount.

Canadian cabinet minister HERB GRAY *in 1995, on learning that he had placed fourth in a* Hill Times *poll on Parliament Hill's sexiest legislators*

Uh, no relation.

Canadian justice minister ALLAN ROCK's *game reply in 1995 when asked by a reporter if he knew anything about a feud between two Quebec motorcycle gangs, the Rock Machine and the Rockers*

When a psychologist or psychiatrist testifies during a defendant's competency hearing, the psychologist or psychiatrist shall wear a cone-shaped hat that is not less than two feet tall. The surface of the hat shall be imprinted with stars and lightning bolts.

Additionally, the psychologist or psychiatrist shall be required to don a white beard that is not less than eighteen inches in length, and shall punctuate crucial elements in his testimony by stabbing the air with a wand.

Whenever a psychologist or psychiatrist provides expert testimony regarding the defendant's testimony, the bailiff shall dim the courtroom lights and administer two strikes to a Chinese gong.

From an amendment proposed in 1995 by DUNCAN SCOTT, *a New Mexico state senator, to a bill addressing the state's licensing guidelines for psychologists and psychiatrists. Scott, a Republican, intended to draw attention to the rise of "insanity pleas in criminal trials." The amendment was approved by the state senate but rejected by the New Mexico House of Representatives.*

Do I let a group of power-mongering men with short penises tell me what to do?

> DORIS ALLEN, *speaker of the California state assembly, in 1995, on her fellow Republicans' attempts to have her recalled*

I apologize for this voice. In fact, if you don't like any of my answers, I may break both your kneecaps.

> *California governor* PETE WILSON *in 1995, suffering a raspy voice after surgery, doing a Godfather impression at a meeting of GOPAC, the Republican political action committee*

The Congressional Circus

No, my dear. In the Senate, maybe, but not in the House.

> *President* GROVER CLEVELAND, *who quarreled with Senate leaders but got on with most members of the House of Representatives, on being awakened by his wife, who cried, "There are burglars in the house."*

The more we remove penalties for being a bum, the more bumism is going to blossom.

> *Senator* JESSE HELMS *on the pointlessness of welfare and other measures to help the poor. After all, as Helms noted, "A lot of human beings have been born bums."*

I'm a sweet grandmother capable of impaling.

> CARRIE MEEK, 66, *newly elected congresswoman from Miami, in 1992, on her political style*

The debates of that great assembly are frequently vague and perplexed, seeming to be dragged rather than to march to the intended goal. Something of this sort must, I think, always happen in public democratic assemblies.

ALEXIS DE TOCQUEVILLE

—————————————— ♦ ——————————————

Tudors Needed.

Florida representative JIM BACCHUS, *in a 1992 letter to House colleagues recruiting tutors for underachieving high school students*

We didn't send you to Washington to make intelligent decisions. We sent you to represent us.

KENT YORK, *a Texas Baptist pastor, in 1993, on Representative Bill Sarpalius's vote for the Clinton administration's first budget*

The president's second-born, golf every weekend, a new aircraft carrier named the USS DeConcini. . . . And you know Grand Canyon National Park? We're renaming it Dennis Canyon National Park.

White House press secretary DEE DEE MYERS *in 1993, joking about what Arizona senator Dennis DeConcini got in return for voting for the Clinton budget*

He looked at Senator Hatch and said, "I'm going to make her cry, I'm going to sing 'Dixie' until she cries." And I looked at him and said,

"Senator Helms, your singing would make me cry if you sang 'Rock of Ages.'"

> Senator CAROL MOSELEY-BRAUN (D–Ill.) in 1993, on an encounter with Senator Jesse Helms in a Senate elevator. A Helms spokesman said it had been "a good-natured exchange."

Let me adjust my hearing aid. It could not accommodate the decibels of the senator from Massachusetts. I can't match him in decibels, or Jezebels, or anything else, apparently.

> Senator JESSE HELMS in 1993, after Senator Edward Kennedy (D–Mass.) gave a passionate speech in favor of extending U.S. residency to foreigners with AIDS

It's too bad Moses is so wrong on this one.

> Representative NITA LOWEY in 1994, on actor Charlton Heston's opposition to the Clinton administration's proposed assault gun ban

Rather than take a chance of being embarrassed again, I'm going to start buying colored handkerchiefs.

> Senator HOWELL HELFLIN in 1994, after he pulled a pair of his wife's white panties out of his pocket. He had grabbed them by mistake instead of a handkerchief when he left for work.

RESTRICTED PARKING. AUTHORIZED USERS ONLY.

> New sign at Washington, D.C.'s, National Airport, replacing one that read, "Reserved for Members of Congress"

Suppose you were an idiot. And suppose you were a member of Congress. But I repeat myself.

MARK TWAIN

————————————— ♦ —————————————

Couldn't you pipe in C-SPAN?

Representative BARNEY FRANK *(D–Mass.) in 1993, when told of Attorney General Janet Reno's wish for a sleeping gas that could have knocked out the occupants of the Branch Davidian compound near Waco, Texas, then under siege by federal agents*

Basically a dog person. I certainly, though, wouldn't want to offend my constituents who are cat people, and I should say that being, I hope, a sensitive person, that I have nothing against cats, and had cats when I was a boy, and if we didn't have the two dogs, might very well be interested in having a cat now.

Freshman Missouri representative JAMES TALENT *in 1993, on being asked in a Spy magazine prank, "Are you a dog or a cat person?"*

I can't comprehend the mystery of how these porno freaks keep getting this money. . . . Porno jerk Tim Miller got almost $15,000. Holly Hughes, porno female jerk, she got $9,375, Kitchen Theater, porno scum, $20,000. Frameline, porno slime, got almost $20,000. Marlon Riggs, $50,000, used the taxpayers' money from both the NEA [National Endowment for the Arts] and public broadcasting . . . to produce the pornographic, profanity-filled, pro-homosexual documentary *Tongues Untied*—absolute garbage.

> *Representative* ROBERT DORNAN *(R–Calif.) in a 1994 speech in which he proposed cuts to the NEA*

President Clinton had a bill, e–i–e–i–o. And in that bill was lots of pork, e–i–e–i–o.

> *Senator* ALFONSE D'AMATO *(R–N.Y.) in 1994, singing the tune "Old MacDonald" in a speech criticizing the Clinton administration crime bill*

———————— **Reality Check** ————————

The cure for admiring the House of Lords is to go and look at it.

> WALTER BAGEHOT

————————————— ♦ —————————————

The present system may be flawed, but that's not to say that we in Congress can't make it worse.

> *Representative* E. CLAY SHAW *(R–Fla.) in 1994, during the debate on health-care reform*

We've killed health care; now we've got to make sure our fingerprints aren't on it.

> *Senator* BOB PACKWOOD *in 1994, on his party's success in preventing passage of the Clinton administration's health-care reforms*

I'm Chris Dodd, and I'm a Democrat.

Senator CHRISTOPHER DODD *(D–Conn.) in 1994, opening a press conference soon after the Democrats' losses in the midterm elections, mimicking the 12-step program of Alcoholics Anonymous*

———— Reality Check ————

A democracy is a government in the hands of men of low birth, no property, and vulgar employments.

ARISTOTLE

———————— ♦ ————————

It's not true. He was just taking a few moments for deep reflection.

An aide to Representative Martin Hoke (R–Ohio) in 1995, responding to queries suggesting that Hoke, who was seen on the House floor with legs propped on a desk, head back, and eyes closed, had been asleep during a portion of the 100-day debate over elements of the GOP's "Contract With America"

People say, "You are an animal-rights nut." I'm not. But they don't have anybody. An elephant can't come out on the [House or Senate] floor. It doesn't have any Congressmen or Senators to represent it, so somebody has to speak up.

Senator ROBERT C. SMITH *(R–N.H.) in 1995, in a 45-minute soliloquy to try to block the observance of the 125th anniversary of the Ringling Bros. and Barnum & Bailey Circus on the Capitol grounds. "How do you stop an elephant if it goes berserk on the grounds of the Capitol?" Smith asked.*

Reality Check

It is a little amusing to see the stickers that have been worn by so many of my colleagues that say, "Term Limits, Yes." It doesn't say, "Term Limits, Now." It says, "Term Limits, Yes." I'm reminded of the great and famous prayer of St. Augustine, who said: "Dear God, make me pure. But not now."

Representative HENRY HYDE *in 1995, arguing against a term limits law for members of Congress*

◆

[T]hey] drink and bathe in Perrier.

Representative PETE STARK *in 1995, explaining why, in his view, Republicans don't mind cutting the budget for clean water*

They're coming for your children, they're coming for the poor, they're coming for the sick, the elderly, the disabled.

Representative JOHN LEWIS *(D–Ga.) in 1995, comparing GOP lawmakers to Nazi stormtroopers in their efforts to slash social assistance spending*

If this doesn't work, what's next? Castration? Sterilization?

Representative WILLIAM CLAY *(D–Mo.) in 1995, attacking GOP proposals to reduce the number of births out of wedlock by cutting welfare payments to young unwed mothers*

I took the Canal Zone and let Congress debate, and while the debate goes on the canal does also.
>   THEODORE ROOSEVELT on *building the Panama Canal*

──────── ♦ ────────

I've still got a lot to learn about Washington. Why, yesterday I accidentally spent some of my own money.
>   *Senator* FRED THOMPSON *(R–Tenn.) in 1995*

It's like getting your first No. 1 record. You hope and dream all your life, and then it finally happens.
>   *Representative* SONNY BONO *(R–Calif.) in 1995, to Newt Gingrich*
>   *on Gingrich's having become House Speaker*

An important person like Jay Leno sent a cake?
>   *Representative* SONNY BONO *in 1995, exhibiting trademark humility*
>   *on his 60th birthday when "The Tonight Show" sent a camera crew*
>   *bearing a cake*

You all sit down, sit down and shut up! Sit down and shut up!
>   *Representative* SAM GIBBONS *(D–Fla.) in 1995, losing patience with*
>   *GOP lawmakers who were heckling him*

Harry, don't start out with an inferiority complex. For the first six months you'll wonder how the hell you got here, and after that you'll wonder how the hell the rest of us got here.

Advice to freshman congressman Harry Truman in 1934
from Majority Whip HAMILTON ("HAM") LEWIS
of Illinois

◆

If BS was a dollar a pound, we would have paid off the deficit at about noon.

Representative JIM ROSS LIGHTFOOT *(R–Iowa), in 1995, during*
debate on the House balanced budget resolution

No job is beneath me.

Representative MARK FOLEY *(R–Fla.) in 1995, on working in*
Congress after holding blue-collar jobs

I have been up to see the [Confederate] Congress, and they do not seem to be able to do anything except eat peanuts and chew tobacco, while my army is starving.

ROBERT E. LEE *in 1865*

◆

Have you ever thought about the Marilyn Monroe stamp? Imagine putting a loser like that on a stamp. Poor, sweet Marilyn. Slept all over town.

> *Representative* ROBERT DORNAN *(R–Calif.) in 1995, expressing concern about the "cultural meltdown" in family values caused in part by Hollywood, with the collusion of government—including the U.S. Postal Service*

I saw Strom Thurmond come back to life.

> WENDY WASSERSTEIN *in 1995, on the 92-year-old senator's introduction to Hollywood actress Melanie Griffith, who had just wooed congressional conservatives on behalf of the endangered National Endowment for the Humanities*

—————————— **Reality Check** ——————————

[Congressmen are so] damn dumb they could throw themselves on the ground and miss.

> *Frequent saying of Representative* JAMES TRAFICANT JR. *(D–Ohio)*

—————————— ◆ ——————————

If you need to burn something, burn your congressman in effigy.

> *Representative* LINDSEY GRAHAM *(R–South Carolina) in 1995, supporting the flag-burning amendment just before it passed*

Veepdom

I never wanted to be vice president of anything in my life.
> NELSON ROCKEFELLER, *asked if he felt honored to serve as*
> *vice president under Gerald Ford*

God . . . isn't it great? Did you ever see so many cops?
> *Vice President–elect* GEORGE BUSH *in 1980, enjoying a motorcycle*
> *escort in his limousine*

Let us see George Bush reelected this November. And then we'll talk about 1994.
> DAN QUAYLE *in 1992, asked whether he will seek the presidency in*
> *the next election, to be held in 1996*

Office of the Vice President . . . The Council on Competativeness
> *Letterhead on stationery, complete with misspelling, found in Dan*
> *Quayle's old White House office by Clinton administration staffers*
> *in 1993*

I heard you had a lot of power.
> *Atlanta Braves outfielder* RON GANT *in 1993 to a visiting Al Gore,*
> *after watching the vice president heft a bat during warm-ups at a game*
> *where Gore threw out the first pitch*

"Your Adequacy" is okay.
> *Vice President* AL GORE *in 1993, when asked by David Letterman*
> *how he should be addressed*

The vice president simply presides over the Senate and sits around hoping for a funeral. . . . I don't have any ambition to hold an office like that.

Senator HARRY TRUMAN *(D–Mo.), shortly before becoming his party's 1944 nominee for vice president on a ticket with Franklin Roosevelt, whose death only a year later would elevate him to the presidency. At the moment when, in Warm Springs, Georgia, FDR was dying, Truman was indeed ostensibly presiding over a Senate session. In fact, he was passing the time by writing a letter home: "Dear Mama & Mary: I am trying to write you a letter today from the desk of the President of the Senate while a windy Senator . . . is making a speech on a subject with which he is in no way familiar. . . ."*

―――――――――――― ◆ ――――――――――――

Hey lady, what about me?

Vice President AL GORE *in 1993, to a woman who ignored him while asking a question of Representative Joe Kennedy (D–Mass.) at a Boston function*

I asked him to do it because he was the only person that I could trust to read all 150,000 pages in the Code of Federal Regulations.

President BILL CLINTON *in 1995, on Vice President Gore's plans to tackle federal regulatory reform*

Flip-Flop Flaps

[**H**e] so shamelessly put his own self-interest above those of his state
and nation.

> Senator PHIL GRAMM, *then a Democrat, in an unsuccessful bid to*
> *defeat incumbent Lloyd Bentsen in the 1976 primary for the Senate,*
> *faulting Bentsen for flirting with a presidential bid while still serving in*
> *the Senate—a circumstance repeated in Gramm's own effort in*
> *beginning in 1995 to seek both reelection to the Senate from Texas and*
> *the GOP presidential nomination*

What has happened is a lot of people have come to me and said they
think that I really have a duty to do something else, people who are
not just flattering.

> Governor PETE WILSON (R–Calif.) *in early 1995, attempting to*
> *explain why he was condoning efforts on his behalf to begin organizing*
> *a Wilson run for the presidency only a few months after a successful*
> *gubernatorial campaign in which, when asked if he would consider a*
> *presidential run if reelected, flatly said, "I'll rule it out"*

————— Reality Check —————

Promises and pie crust are made to be broken.

JONATHAN SWIFT

♦

The casino plays on greed. The sense of the ultimate chance, the hope against hope that the spin of the wheel or the shoot of the dice will produce instant wealth, instant power, instant gratification. The work ethic, "steady as you go," appears alongside as fundamentally boring, goody two-shoes values.

> BOB RAE, *leader of the New Democratic Party in Ontario, in 1990, restating his party's longstanding opposition to government involvement in gambling. In 1992, after becoming premier of Ontario, Rae approved the introduction of casinos, off-track betting, and sports lotteries as a means of generating revenues to fill an empty provincial treasury.*

But, as one of them climbed up inside the wagon with me, while I was lying on my back, I put a size ten-and-a-half cordovan where I thought it might do some good—and vaulted him back into the street.

> *Law-and-order crusader* PATRICK BUCHANAN, *1992 and 1996 candidate for the GOP presidential nomination, recounting in his autobiography an incident in which, as a 20-year-old student at Washington's Georgetown University, he was stopped by police on a speeding charge and, after protesting, was roughly tossed into a police wagon by one of the officers. He later pleaded guilty to a misdemeanor assault charge.*

I don't suppose you'd want anybody to keep a campaign promise if it was a very unsound policy.

> *Secretary of State* WARREN CHRISTOPHER, *trying to smother embarrassment over another Clinton administration climb-down from a hard-line stance on Bosnia and Haiti by invoking the Clinton record of broken campaign promises*

This is like saying how likely am I to jump over a tall building in a single bound—unlikely. This is like asking is lightning going to strike here in the next two seconds—I don't think so.

> ROSS PEROT *in 1992, on the chances of his resuming his presidential candidacy. A few weeks later, Perot rejoined the race, ultimately capturing 19 percent of the vote.*

. . . **S**uch as Rwanda and Haiti.

Senator JESSE HELMS *in a 1994 letter to the head of the federal Agency for International Development (AID), urging it to maintain roughly $20 million worth of funding for North Carolina State University agricultural research programs on soil management and peanuts in, among other places, Rwanda and Haiti. One of the most consistently outspoken critics of foreign aid, who had just likened it to pouring money down a "rat hole," Helms felt a need to balance this against his home state's status as one of the biggest state beneficiaries of AID spending, which for North Carolina amounted to some $400 million in contracts for goods and services in 1994.*

Cutting these chaplains at this time would have been a symbolic negative because it would say, in so many words, that we don't think religion is that important.

PAUL WEYRICH, *founder of National Empowerment Television, in 1995, on the decision by the new GOP leadership in Congress to back down from a plan to replace two full-time chaplains and their staff— whose salaries totaled $289,000—with volunteer ministers as an economy measure*

Reality Check

No, I look at the senators and pray for the country.

The Senate chaplain, asked in 1903 if he prays for the senators

◆

Ambiguously definitive—or is it definitively ambiguous?
Senator BILL BRADLEY (D–N.J.) *in 1995, acknowledging that he had been less than clear about his presidential ambitions*

The Dismal Science

The United States should adopt a protective tariff of such a character as will help the struggling industries of Europe get on their feet.
President WARREN HARDING, *exhibiting a peculiar grasp of trade policy, by whose conventions a protective tariff would more likely have the effect of punishing industries in foreign lands. Admittedly infirm in economic matters, Harding once interrupted himself from his struggles in responding to a taxation proposal, moaning to a White House secretary, "Somewhere there must be a book that tells all about it, where I could go to straighten it out in my mind. But I don't know where the book is, and maybe I couldn't read it if I found it. . . . My God, this is a hell of a place for a man like me to be!"*

[I have] saved America from inflation.
President HERBERT HOOVER, *finding a silver lining in the onset of the Great Depression*

Blessed are the young, for they shall inherit the national debt.
President HERBERT HOOVER

What makes a businessman tick? God, I hate the bastards.
President JOHN KENNEDY, *son of a millionaire businessman, during a dispute with steel industry leaders*

Limit nonrecognition treatment when securities are received in certain Section 351 transactions.

> *Bureaucratise for a $1.5 billion tax increase over five years in a 1989 bill signed by President George Bush*

Canada must throw Keynes right out the window.

> JACQUES PARIZEAU, *Parti Québécois finance minister, addressing a gathering of federal and provincial finance ministers. Federal finance minister Jean Chrétien responded, "Dat's okay with me. I never knew dis Keynes guy anyway. Let's throw him out and get on with the meeting."*

Now is the time to kill the Taxasaurus monster! Kill the dinosaur, kill him now! If you don't, he's going to eat more jobs. So take this lead pencil and give him lead poisoning. Kill him!

> *Senator* ALFONSE D'AMATO *in 1993, during the debate on President Clinton's first budget. Known affectionately to his constituents as "Senator Pothole," D'Amato had justly earned a reputation as a channeler of prodigious amounts of federal pork into New York State generally and his Long Island neighborhood in particular.*

The president's upstairs having a drink and a cigar and will make that decision shortly.

> ROGER ALTMAN, *deputy treasury secretary, in 1993, when asked if higher "sin taxes" on liquor and tobacco would be among the means of financing health-care reforms*

I'm standing in the kitchen and having my wife throw pots and pans at me.

> ROBERT REISCHAUER, *congressional budget office director, in 1994, on his preparations for testifying to Congress on the Clinton health-care plan*

Not as a stimulus package.

> *Senator* BOB KERREY *in 1993, on whether he was still dating actress Debra Winger. The veiled reference was to President Clinton's $19.5 billion economic-incentive program, or "stimulus package," which was stymied by the GOP in the Senate.*

How's That Again?

We must prosper America first.

> *President* WARREN HARDING, *former small-town Ohio newspaper editor, exhibiting a novel concept of sentence structure*

Progression is not proclamation or palaver. It is not pretense nor play on prejudice. It is not of personal pronouns, nor perennial pronouncement. It is not the perturbation of a people passion-wrought, nor a promise proposed.

> *President* WARREN HARDING, *master of alliteration. Contemporary journalist H. L. Mencken of the Baltimore Sunpapers said Harding's oratory called to mind "dogs barking idiotically through endless nights. It is so bad a sort of grandeur creeps into it."*

If Lincoln were alive today he'd roll over in his grave.

President GERALD FORD

The specificity of the totality.

Canadian political leader JOE CLARK

That is true—but not absolutely true.

JEAN DRAPEAU, longtime mayor of Montreal, asked if his czaristic approach to governing possibly reminded him of Lord Acton's dictum that "power tends to corrupt, and absolute power corrupts absolutely"

--------- **Reality Check** ---------

I'm one of those mayors whose management style is to allow free and unlimited debate, to a point.

MARION BARRY, mayor of Washington, D.C., in 1987

———————————— ♦ ————————————

What you have here is an Administration that has set its hair on fire and is trying to put it out with a hammer.

Senator ALFONSE D'AMATO in 1988, on the Reagan administration's failed attempt to oust Panamanian dictator Manuel Noriega

I became adept at pronounless sentences, I did. Instead of
"I moved to Texas and soon we joined the Republican
party," it was, "Moved to Texas, joined the Republican
party, raised a family . . ." Imagined him raising his hand on
the Capitol steps—"Do solemnly swear, will preserve and
protect . . ."

White House speechwriter PEGGY NOONAN *in 1990, on*
adjusting to George Bush's style after working for
Ronald Reagan

◆

I am less interested in what the definition is. You might argue
technically, are we in a recession or not. But when there's this kind of
sluggishness and concern—definitions, heck with it.

President GEORGE BUSH *in 1991, on reports of gathering*
economic gloom

The defense budget is more than a piggy bank for people who want to
get busy beating swords into pork barrels.

President GEORGE BUSH *in 1992, campaigning at a high-tech robotics*
plant in Anaheim, California

I see no media mention of it, but we entered in—you asked what time
it is and I'm telling you how to build a watch here—but we had Boris
Yeltsin here the other day. And I think of my times campaigning in
Iowa, years ago, and how there was a—Iowa has a kind of, I single out

Iowa, it's kind of an international state in a sense and has a great interest in all these things—and we had Yeltsin standing here in the Rose Garden, and we entered into a deal to eliminate the biggest and most threatening ballistic missiles . . . and it was almost, "Ho-hum, what have you done for me lately?"

> President GEORGE BUSH in 1992, defending his record as president
> on "CBS This Morning."

Hawaii is a unique state. It is a small state. It is a state that is by itself. It is a—it is different than the other states. Well, *all* states are different, but it's got a particularly unique situation.

> Vice President DAN QUAYLE in 1992, disputing Bill Clinton's
> assertion that Hawaii's universal health-care system was a worthy
> model for national health-care reforms

The more I think about the project, the more I like the general karma of it if the finances can be worked out.

> Governor WILLIAM WELD of Massachusetts in 1993, on a proposed
> museum of contemporary art planned for North
> Adams, Massachusetts

Elvis is in fact a Republican.

> House budget chief JOHN KASICH (R–Ohio) in 1995. Presley once
> did accept a job as an anti-drugs spokesman from Richard Nixon,
> suggesting that if, as many believe, Elvis is alive, Kasich may be on
> to something.

You can now get a certificate to teach German by sitting through enough classes, but if you speak German, you can't teach German if you don't have a certificate. So you can have a German teacher who can't speak German, but though they have the certificate so they can teach, even though they can't teach . . . If you can speak it, you can't teach it, even if you could teach it. Are you with me so far?

NEWT GINGRICH

I am wearing a dinosaur tie today, and I did it deliberately. . . . And it occurred to me—I want to make two points about this dinosaur tie. This is a—I think a tyrannosaurus—I mean a triceratops, coming out of the egg. The first point I want to make is that they're extinct and that you could take that as a sort of warning to us that these things happen. The second point I want to make is that they're extinct and that in fact life is like that. . . . I think on the one hand when people say, you know, let's preserve X, well, my first point is going to be if at some point in the next 50,000 years the Earth tilts, as it will—at least it has now so far for its entire history—that slight tilt will change totally the ecosystem you're prepared currently to spend endless quantities to save. At that point the Sahara may well once again bloom as it used to and you may have new deserts in areas that are now wet, and that's in fact the nature of history over time. . . . Now, I'd love to see what a troglodyte would be like if it were alive, but I'm not sure that in and of itself that ought to be the end point. . . . Are people a part of that ecosystem or are people in fact aliens?

NEWT GINGRICH in 1995, on "The Role of Man in Nature versus What Is the Role of Man in Nature"

· 3 ·

Bill Clinton and the Stature Gap

Well, I don't have much job security.

BILL CLINTON *in 1992, on why he still plays the saxophone*

When you're starting to have a good time, you're supposed to be someplace else. . . . When someone tells you it's not personal, they're fixing to stick it to you. . . . Nearly everyone will lie to you, given the right circumstances.

Presidential candidate BILL CLINTON, *in conversation with a* New York Times *reporter on his campaign plane in 1992*

Mr. Bush says the election should be about trust, and I believe that's right. But for George Bush to say the election should be about trust is like me saying it should be about short speeches.

BILL CLINTON, *campaigning for the presidency in 1992*

Goodbye.

> *The entirety of a speech by President* CALVIN
> COOLIDGE, *whose circumspection stands in contrast to
> the verbosity of current political figures such as Bill
> Clinton and Newt Gingrich, whose tendency to go on at
> length is a syndrome known to communications therapists
> as "flooding"*

———————————— ♦ ————————————

Whooooooo, Pig! Soooooooie!

> BILL CLINTON *in 1992, demonstrating his hog-calling skills on the
> campaign trail in Tennessee*

After the election . . . there'll be nobody to make fun of.

> BILL CLINTON, *campaigning in 1992*

I won my age and body-fat division.

> BILL CLINTON *in 1992, after finishing with an unflattering time in a
> 5-kilometer Thanksgiving Day race in Little Rock*

Stuff.

> *President-elect* BILL CLINTON *in 1992, answering a reporter who
> asked what he had been working on*

The chart you had was very moving.

President-elect BILL CLINTON *in 1992, at his economic summit, referring to a chart showing the difference in wages earned by college- and high-school-educated workers*

Deep down inside I wanted to say it the way I was thinking it: "So . . . Help me, God."

BILL CLINTON *in 1993, on his thoughts while delivering the traditional "So help me God" closing to his oath of office*

I don't necessarily consider McDonald's junk food. You know, they have chicken sandwiches, they have salads . . .

BILL CLINTON *in 1993, defending his weakness for McDonald's fare*

One of you might trip over it and break a leg. Then you'd sue us and it would run up the deficits.

BILL CLINTON *in 1993, stopping the line of visitors at his White House open house while a rug was being taped down*

I didn't misspeak myself. Nothing I said is in any way inconsistent with anything I've ever said before about this.

BILL CLINTON *in 1993, on his comment that homosexuals might be excluded from some duty assignments in the military, an apparent reversal of his gays-in-the-military policy. HIV-positive presidential adviser Bob Hattoy's response: "If you apply what [Clinton] has said to civilian life, you'd be restricting gays and lesbians to jobs as florists and hairdressers."*

When the Japanese say "Yes" to us they often mean "No."

> BILL CLINTON *to Russian president Boris Yeltsin at a 1993 summit in*
> *Vancouver. Asked if it were true that the Japanese often mean "No"*
> *when they say "Yes," Japanese government spokesperson Tohei Kono*
> *said, "No."*

We're Eisenhower Republicans here, and we are fighting the Reagan Republicans. We stand for lower deficits and free trade and the bond market. Isn't that great?

> *A discouraged* BILL CLINTON *in 1993, protesting to advisers that his*
> *proposed economic stimulus program to create jobs immediately was*
> *being held hostage by Wall Street*

You mean to tell me that the success of the program and my reelection hinges on the Federal Reserve and a bunch of f——g bond traders?

> *Attributed to President-elect* BILL CLINTON *in* The Agenda, *Bob*
> *Woodward's 1994 chronicle of the Clinton White House, on being*
> *advised to focus his efforts on deficit reduction rather than new*
> *social programs*

Come on, come on. Listen, goddammit. You can't do that. You can't bring me out here with the mayor and a congresswoman and push them back.

> BILL CLINTON *in 1993, reaming out an aide who blocked*
> *Washington, D.C., mayor Sharon Pratt Kelly and D.C.*
> *congressional delegate Eleanor Holmes Norton from joining him in a*
> *photo opportunity with local construction workers*

He tried to burn it in there. I decided the main thing was to get it to the catcher.

> BILL CLINTON *in 1993, comparing his soft but accurate pitch to open the baseball season with George Bush's off-line bouncer the previous year*

———— Reality Check ————

I used to think if there was reincarnation, I wanted to come back as the president or a .400 baseball hitter. But now I want to come back as the bond market. You can intimidate everybody.

> JAMES CARVILLE, *campaign strategist to Bill Clinton, in 1993*

———— ♦ ————

I'm glad nobody found out about that manicure I got in California.

> BILL CLINTON *in 1993, referring to the uproar over the pricey haircut he received on Air Force One*

He just resents it because Mack's a short guy with real power.

> BILL CLINTON *in 1993, on Ross Perot's insistence that White House chief of staff Mack McLarty, former CEO of a pipeline company, is not a "real" businessperson*

I don't hate anyone. I forget the people I'm supposed to hate.

> *Attributed to* BILL CLINTON *in* The Agenda, *in response to a London newspaper report that said Clinton hated British prime minister John Major*

I always say I don't know whether it's the finest public housing in America or the crown jewel of the prison system.

BILL CLINTON in 1993, on life in the White House

I made my lowest grade in conduct, because I talked too much in school and the teachers were always telling me to stop talking.

BILL CLINTON in 1993

I thought to myself, "That was a pretty good speech, but not good enough to give twice."

BILL CLINTON in 1993, on what went through his mind when an old speech to Congress initially flashed up on the TelePrompTer as he began his health-care address to Congress

You guys resting?

BILL CLINTON in 1993, to former presidents George Bush, Jimmy Carter, and Gerald Ford, after they asked for chairs during a prolonged Clinton speech on the North American Free Trade Agreement

─────────── **Reality Check** ───────────

If I am to speak ten minutes, I need a week for preparation; if 15 minutes, three days; if half an hour, two days; if an hour, I am ready now.

President WOODROW WILSON, when asked by a cabinet officer how long it took him to prepare his admirably concise speeches

───────── ◆ ─────────

I've got to be more like John Wayne.

BILL CLINTON *in 1993, agreeing with his new image adviser David Gergen that he must try to look more presidential*

It was a real sort of Southern deal. I had AstroTurf in the back. You don't want to know why, but I did.

> BILL CLINTON, *reminiscing about an El Camino pickup truck he once owned, while visiting a GM plant in Louisiana in 1994. "I carried my luggage back there," Clinton said later. "It wasn't for what everybody thought it was for when I made the comment. . . . I'm guilty of a lot of things, but I didn't ever do that."*

I grew up in a little town in Arkansas that had a substantial Lithuanian population. So I grew up knowing about the problems of Baltic nations.

> BILL CLINTON *in 1994, prior to a visit to Latvia, on the foreign affairs knowledge he picked up around the neighborhood in Hope, Arkansas*

I was thinking of you last night, Helmut, because I watched the sumo wrestling on television. You and I are the biggest people here and we're still 100 pounds too light.

> BILL CLINTON *in 1994, to German chancellor Helmut Kohl at a NATO meeting in Brussels*

He's not going anywhere. He's my best friend.

> BILL CLINTON *in 1994, on former chief of staff Mack McLarty, who had just been reassigned*

Can I answer every question that anybody might ever ask me about something that happened 10, 15, 17 years ago on the spur of the moment and have total recall of that while trying to be president? No sir, I cannot.

BILL CLINTON in 1994, responding to an editor who said his Whitewater explanations seemed evasive

Usually briefs.

BILL CLINTON in a 1994 MTV town meeting, responding to an audience member who asked if the president wore briefs or boxer shorts

Maybe I'm just not as good a talker as you folks thought I was when I got elected.

BILL CLINTON in 1994, asked about his low public approval ratings

Five percent? No one can be that low.

BILL CLINTON in 1994, on the low public approval rating for Polish president Lech Walesa

Pray for me.

BILL CLINTON in 1994, addressing parishioners at a Maryland church, asking for divine help with passage of his crime bill

Bless you.

BILL CLINTON in 1994, responding to a questioner at a town hall meeting who said, "Whitewater is for canoeing and rafting"

I am not sure what speech is in the TelePrompTer tonight, but I hope we can talk about the State of the Union.

BILL CLINTON *in 1994, referring to his last Congressional address, when the wrong speech was loaded into the machine*

I think I've lost reelection in 1996 already, but we've been waiting so long for this game it'll be worth it.

BILL CLINTON *in 1994, joking about his support for the NCAA champion Arkansas Razorbacks*

I'm used to these seven-game stretches. That seems like the story of my career, so I identify with you guys. You didn't choke.

BILL CLINTON *in a 1994 congratulatory telephone call to the Stanley Cup champion New York Rangers*

Term limits are looking better to me each day.

BILL CLINTON *in 1994, in the aftermath of the elections in which the GOP took control of both houses of Congress*

God knows what she could've gotten my mother to say.

BILL CLINTON *to Newt Gingrich in 1995, after Gingrich's mother told Connie Chung that her son had referred to Hillary Rodham Clinton as "a bitch"*

He says he regrets any mistakes he has made. So do I.

BILL CLINTON *in 1995, on allegations of ethical transgressions facing his housing secretary Henry Cisneros*

The economy has produced 6.1 million jobs since I became President and if Michael Jordan comes back to the Bulls, it will be 6,100,001 jobs.

> BILL CLINTON *in 1995. Dave Anderson, sports columnist in* The New York Times, *reminded Clinton that the basketball star had given up a short-lived career in minor-league baseball in order to rejoin the Bulls. "The President didn't dare say, 'Oops, I forgot to subtract the baseball job he had. I guess it's still 6.1 million jobs.' "*

Why yes, I am a rocket scientist.

> *Jogging T-shirt favored by Bill Clinton in the spring of 1995*

"Life is like a box of chocolates. You never know what you're gonna get." Maybe that's why I never liked chocolate.

> BILL CLINTON *in 1995, citing a truism from the movie* Forrest Gump, *a few weeks after his party lost control of both houses of Congress. Clinton is allergic to chocolate.*

The Clinton Watch

Bill Clinton writes that Chelsea's ballet skills have reached a new level of perfection. . . . Bill notes that in early November he was elected President of the United States.

> ROBERT REICH, *labor secretary in the Clinton administration and a fellow Rhodes Scholar of Clinton, in a contribution to the class of 1968 class-notes section of the latest* American Oxonian, *the Rhodes Scholar alumni magazine*

What a dweeb. He did not even have his windows down.

> RAMONA JOYCE, *inaugural parade spectator, in 1993, after Bill Clinton drove by her section in a closed car with tinted windows*

We spent enormous amounts of time trying to teach him.

> *A friend of Bill Clinton's youth, explaining in David Maraniss's 1995 Clinton biography* First in His Class *that the future president, who never smoked cigarettes, did indeed appear incapable of inhaling marijuana*

He talked about how he was a fat kid when he was 5 and 6, and how the other kids taunted him.

> *A Washington Post source reporting on what Bill Clinton talked about at a Camp David "human-resource development" exercise conducted by "facilitators" to encourage bonding among cabinet members*

---------------- **Reality Check** ----------------

You can go ahead. I am the large party.

> *President* WILLIAM TAFT *to a conductor upon boarding a train which he had asked be made to stop at that spot to take on "a large party." Taft weighed about 300 pounds.*

---------------- ◆ ----------------

Bill, I'm on long distance, so I'll just call you back.

> DENNIS BYRD, *partially paralyzed New York Jets player, in 1992, answering Bill Clinton's get-well telephone call. Byrd thought the call was a prank.*

He's a 44 long. I can tell you by looking at him.

> *Tailor* RALPH ESPOSITO *in 1993, after seeing Bill Clinton Christmas*
> *shopping at Saks Fifth Avenue in New York City*

I am not saying this in a negative way. But honestly, do you really think that Hillary or Bill Clinton, from what you can see, is very concerned about their appearance?

> *Hollywood hairdresser* CHRISTOPHE *in 1993, on his two*
> *celebrity clients*

I would have given it more of an oval look. If you look at it, the top of his head looks pointed.

> MILTON PITTS, *former White House barber, in 1993, on Bill*
> *Clinton's new haircut*

He's the one with the white legs.

> *A California woman in 1992, pointing out Bill Clinton for a friend as*
> *the president-elect played volleyball on a Santa Barbara beach*

Meeting him, shaking his hand—it was overwhelming. It was better than sex. Of course, I haven't had sex before, but I'm sure this was better.

> *High-schooler* TYLER PETERSON, *a Boys Nation delegate, in 1993,*
> *after meeting Bill Clinton at the White House*

All celebrated people lose on a close view.

NAPOLEON

———————————— ◆ ————————————

He's at his best when the number of miles he jogs is greater than the number of hours he sleeps.

> *White House counsellor* DAVID GERGEN *in 1993, on a tired Bill Clinton, who had missed his morning jog during a Tokyo visit*

You've got to wear your unpopularity—and I told Clinton this— you've got to wear your unpopularity as a badge of honor.

> *Canadian prime minister* BRIAN MULRONEY *in 1993, after talking with Bill Clinton about opinion polls*

I hope I don't have to. I hope he's on Mount Rushmore in 1996.

> ROSS PEROT *in 1993, asked if he will run for president again, on Bill Clinton*

The typical American boy with no sex appeal. Who would want to look at him? He's full of vitamins and has a face that doesn't say anything.

> BARBARA ALBERTI, *Italian newspaper columnist, in 1994, on Bill Clinton in a survey of women assessing the assertiveness of noted political leaders*

He was like a teddy bear. I didn't want to let him go.

TARSHA THOMAS, 14, in 1994, who asked for, and got, a hug from Bill Clinton when he visited her inner-city school in Washington, D.C.

Shaking hands with Bill Clinton is, in and of itself, a full-body sexual experience, I promise you. He has the sexiest handshake of any man that I have ever experienced in my life.

Author JUDITH KRANTZ in 1994, after meeting the president

─────────────── **Reality Check** ───────────────

A little flattery will support a man through great fatigue.

President JAMES MONROE, on being asked at a White House reception, "Are you not completely worn out?"

───────────────── ◆ ─────────────────

Hooters Welcomes President Clinton.

Sign outside a racy Rhode Island nightspot as the president's motorcade sped by on its way to a health-care event

Bill Clinton is not my commander in chief.

OLIVER NORTH, Virginia senatorial candidate and former Marine, in 1994, arguing that an Iraqi military build-up could be blamed on Clinton-era defense cutbacks

Mr. Clinton better watch out if he comes down here. He'd better have a bodyguard.

> *Senator* JESSE HELMS *of North Carolina in 1994, saying the president's draft record and policies on cuts to military spending and gays in uniform have angered servicemen*

Are you one of us middle-class people, or are you in with the villainous, money-grubbing Republicans?

> REBECCA FAIRCHILD, *a participant in a 1994 town hall meeting, questioning Bill Clinton about his Whitewater investment deal*

Tell the president I'll call him back.

> NEWT GINGRICH *in 1994, two days after the GOP swept to power in Congressional elections, snubbing Bill Clinton*

Nothing was said when I first moved in, and there are no signs that it was his. He didn't carve his name in the furniture.

> EMMA CALDWELL, *an Oxford law student, in 1994, expressing surprise on learning that Bill Clinton had once occupied her dorm room*

If one's attention is immediately drawn to a tie, that is a very good sign that it is a bad tie. The president has made a strong argument that his achievements have gone unnoticed by the American people. That is because they are staring at his ties.

> JIM CICCONI, *former Bush administration official and partner in the law firm of Akin, Gump, Strauss, Hauer & Feld, in 1995*

He was feeling very short of breath. I saw visible palpitations and I saw a great deal of anxiety on the face of the president . . . last night during the game with Syracuse.

White House press secretary MIKE MCCURRY *in 1995, pausing for effect when asked about Bill Clinton's health on a rare day when the president failed to jog. The reference was to a college basketball semifinal contest between Syracuse and Clinton's beloved Arkansas Razorbacks.*

It's always a privilege to introduce someone who also speaks with an accent.

HENRY KISSINGER *in 1995, introducing a foreign policy speech by Bill Clinton*

It's a day care center—children's hour. It's a chaotic White House that's probably in part reflective of the mind of the president of the United States.

PATRICK BUCHANAN *in 1995, on the preponderance of thirtysomething staffers in the Clinton administration*

I think most of us have learned some time ago that if you don't like the president's position on a particular issue, you simply need to wait a few weeks.

Representative ROBERT L. LIVINGSTON (R.-*Louisiana*) *in 1995, on Bill Clinton's about-face in adopting the GOP's budget-balancing rhetoric*

Wouldn't it be funny if, of all the candidates, Bill Clinton had the best marriage?

> JAY LENO *in 1995, observing that in contrast to Clinton, "family values" proponents Bob Dole, Newt Gingrich, Phil Gramm, and Pete Wilson had each divorced and remarried*

[Bill Clinton is] going to try to expand his lead on female voters, one woman at a time.

> ALEX CASTELLANOS, *media adviser to Phil Gramm, in 1995, on the president's image as a womanizer*

The Clinton Crowd Rushes In

We wanted to make sure that we chose a cross section of people and performers that would, to the extent possible, represent every sector of society.

> SALLY AMAN, *spokeswoman for the Inaugural Parade Committee, in 1992, on why the parade would include two Elvis impersonators and a precision lawn chair marching team*

He has to have talent. He can't just be the president's brother.

> AHMET ERTEGUN, *head of Atlantic Records, in 1992, on negotiations with First Brother Roger Clinton on a recording contract. At Esquire magazine, deputy managing editor David Hirshey, who asked Roger Clinton to write an article, said: "He can't just have talent. He has to be the president's brother."*

Headache.
Secret Service code name for First Brother Roger Clinton

F—k him. He gave me a bad grade in law school.
Attributed to a Clinton transition staffer, in nixing the 1993 proposed appointment of one of his former law school professors to a Justice Department post

We do realize here it is important to be careful because we are only tenants.
White House spokeswoman LORRAINE VOLES *in 1993, in a memo asking staffers to keep lids on coffee cups due to the many stains found on rugs in the official residence*

Hey, this is the '90s. We're against killing trees.
White House press secretary DEE DEE MYERS *in 1993, on why the Clinton health-care plan was distributed on computer disks instead of paper*

We made every effort not to scare them.
JERRY GARCIA, *leader of the rock group Grateful Dead, in 1992, on the treatment received by Al and Tipper Gore when they attended the group's Washington concert*

I don't need the leg room.

Labor Secretary ROBERT REICH, *who is less than 5 feet tall, in 1993, on why he doesn't mind flying economy class to comply with Bill Clinton's cost-cutting directives*

—————— **Reality Check** ——————

If you keep dead still, they will run down in three or four minutes.

Ex-president CALVIN COOLIDGE, *advising his successor Herbert Hoover on how to get rid of long-winded visitors to the White House*

————————— ♦ —————————

I can only deal with one nightmare at a time.

White House communications director MARK GEARAN *in 1993, asked about the troubled status of Bobby Rae Inman's nomination as defense secretary at a time when the administration was mired in controversy over the Whitewater investigation and a suggestion by Surgeon General Joycelyn Elders that a study be done on whether the use of marijuana and other illicit drugs should be legalized*

—————— **Reality Check** ——————

Every time I fill a vacant office I make ten malcontents and one ingrate.

LOUIS XIV

————————— ♦ —————————

If I could be the condom queen and get every young person in the United States who is engaging in sex to use a condom, I would wear a crown on my head with a condom on it.

> *Surgeon General* JOYCELYN ELDERS *in 1994*

I'll be delighted to take your questions now, except any questions that relate to the fair-market value of long underwear.

> MARGARET RICHARDSON, *head of the Internal Revenue Service, at a 1994 press conference that came a few days after reports that Bill Clinton took deductions for donations of his underwear*

It looks more like the New York subway system, and I don't think it represents our health-care plan at all.

> *White House chief of staff* MACK MCLARTY *in 1994, on the complex chart the GOP unveiled after Clinton's State of the Union address to oppose the administration's health-care reform proposals*

Welcome to my life.

> GEORGE STEPHANOPOULOS, *White House adviser, in 1994, to his date as press and autograph seekers surrounded them at a Kennedy Center event*

Four Heinekens and . . . nothing else.

> GEORGE STEPHANOPOULOS, *White House adviser and Washington, D.C.'s, most eligible bachelor, in 1994, when asked to describe the contents of his refrigerator*

Not with this president.

> DONNA SHALALA, *secretary of health and human services, in 1994,*
> *to a town hall meeting participant who suggested a "Twinkie tax" on*
> *junk food to help finance universal health care*

I don't comment on pending prosecutions—I mean, well, pending investigations.

> *Attorney General* JANET RENO *in 1994, when asked to comment on*
> *reports that Representative Dan Rostenkowski faced indictment for*
> *abusing his office*

I really can't pronounce his name, but it is something like "Cheese Nachos."

> *Attempt to identify HUD Secretary Henry Cisneros by a C–Span*
> *caller, as related in 1995 by Cisneros himself*

"Chick" would be a welcome improvement.

> CAROL BROWNER, *much-criticized director of the Environmental*
> *Protection Agency, questioned in a 1995 Washington Post survey*
> *that asked if being called a "chick" is demeaning*

He's promised us at least one conjugal visit a month.

> *Newly appointed White House press secretary* MIKE MCCURRY *in*
> *1995, reassuring his pregnant wife that the president wouldn't let long*
> *working hours interfere overly in their private life*

· 4 ·

The Hillary Factor

I will get you, my pretty, and your little dog too.

Caption on a picture of Hillary Clinton portrayed as the Wicked Witch from The Wizard of Oz in the office of Mary Matalin, chief spokesperson for George Bush's presidential reelection campaign, in 1992

If Reaganomics works at all, Whitewater could become the Western Hemisphere's mecca.

> HILLARY CLINTON *in a 1981 letter to business partner James McDougal, on prospects for the future First Family's ill-fated investment in an Arkansas real estate development*

I've never known Jerry not to speak when Jerry wanted to speak. He's always speaking as far as I can tell.

> HILLARY CLINTON *in 1992, on Jerry Brown's efforts to obtain prime-time speaking slots at the Democratic National Convention*

Young man, I want to see you after this rally.

> BILL CLINTON *in 1992, joking to an Iowa supporter who held up a sign that said, "Hillary Is a Babe"*

—————————— **Reality Check** ——————————

We don't want Eleanor either.

> *Message on an anti-FDR campaign button distributed by supporters of FDR presidential rival Wendell Wilkie in 1940*

————————————— ◆ —————————————

Until you've lived through a White House Easter Egg Hunt, you don't know what hell is.

> MERRIE SPAETH, *former aide to First Lady Nancy Reagan, in 1992, on the duties facing the new First Lady, who at the turn of the new year was now referred to as Hillary Rodham Clinton*

HILLARY KNOWS BEST

Message on the T-shirt that Nebraska senator Bob Kerrey wore while jogging with Bill Clinton in June 1993. Kerrey's prospects of being selected as Clinton's running mate in 1992 dimmed when Hillary Clinton allegedly nixed the idea.

When the president called for sacrifice and asked everybody at the White House to give him a 25% cut, I decided to go for a 50% cut and do my part.

HILLARY RODHAM CLINTON in 1993, on her new, shorter hairstyle

We just screwed all these people.

HILLARY RODHAM CLINTON in 1993, pointing out to her husband the crowds still waiting outside as time for the White House open house ran out

I thought you were real people.

HILLARY RODHAM CLINTON in 1993, after disinviting a crowd of spectators to a White House reception after the swearing-in of Supreme Court Justice Ruth Bader Ginsburg when she learned they were members of the press. "The problem is," said a disinvited reporter, "she means it."

We've made a lot of progress on, you know, pasta and things like that—but tofu has been hard for us.

HILLARY RODHAM CLINTON in 1993, on the difficulties of improving her husband's diet

Hardly anybody likes green peas.

HILLARY RODHAM CLINTON *in 1993, on why she deleted "peas" from the "Sesame Street" script she taped a week earlier, and instead advised children to "eat your broccoli, string beans, and apples." Defending the vegetable, NBC anchorman Tom Brokaw said, "Mrs. Clinton, all we are saying is, give peas a chance."*

She should . . . have a serious talk with Denis Thatcher. He knew how to behave.

Sir BERNARD INGHAM, *press secretary to ex-British prime minister Margaret Thatcher, in 1993, offering Hillary Rodham Clinton tips on First Spouse decorum. Mr. Thatcher famously kept a half step behind his wife at all times.*

She would always drive and I would always have to sit in the back.

HUGH RODHAM, *Florida gubernatorial candidate, in 1994, on the pretend rocketship he shared as a kid with his sister, Hillary Rodham Clinton*

"**Y**ou're too old, you can't see, and you're a woman. Maybe the 'dogs' would take you."

HILLARY RODHAM CLINTON *in 1994, repeating how a Marine recruiter dismissed her 1975 effort to enlist. "Dogs" apparently meant the Army.*

Health care amounts to 14% of our GNP—a lot of money. It is the size of the Italian economy. And the president turned it over to his wife.

> JACK KEMP, *former pro-football player, congressman, and Bush administration cabinet officer, in 1994, opposing the Clinton health-care proposals*

What did the president know, and when did Hillary tell him?

> Senator ALFONSE D'AMATO *in 1994, paraphrasing the famous question asked of Watergate witnesses to explain his view of the issues in the probe of the Clintons' Whitewater real-estate investments*

I wouldn't stand too close to her.

> ROGER AILES, *former GOP consultant, in 1994, noting that of the three lawyers brought into the White House on Hillary Rodham Clinton's advice, one committed suicide, one had resigned, and the other was under investigation*

This is the same publication that said she adopted a space-alien baby. If they already have a space-alien baby, I don't know if they need another one.

> NEEL LATTIMORE, *spokesman for Hillary Rodham Clinton, in 1994, denying a report in a tabloid newspaper that the First Lady was pregnant*

As my wife pointed out, I could have gotten neither of these things on my own. I had to be elected president to do it—with her help.

> BILL CLINTON *in 1994, accepting an honorary degree and fellowship at University College, Oxford, where he was a Rhodes Scholar but did not graduate*

If you ever have a traffic accident in Norway, count your blessings.

HILLARY RODHAM CLINTON *in 1994, on the good-looking policemen assigned to her as security guards during her visit to the Winter Olympics at Lillehammer, Norway*

Being a Cubs fan prepares you for life—and Washington.

HILLARY RODHAM CLINTON *in 1994, on how rooting for her hometown Chicago Cubs baseball team has made her philosophical about adversity*

———————— **Reality Check** ————————

In the Bible it says they asked Jesus how many times you should forgive, and he said 70 times 7. Well, I want you all to know that I'm keeping a chart.

HILLARY RODHAM CLINTON *in a 1994 speech at the National Prayer Luncheon*

——————————— ◆ ———————————

The reports of your charm are overstated, and the reports of your wit are understated.

Representative RICHARD ARMEY *(R–Tex.), House majority leader, in conversation with First Lady Hillary Rodham Clinton*

This is a chick trip.

CBS news correspondent MARTHA TEICHNER *in 1995, on why a male colleague was excluded from Hillary Rodham Clinton's goodwill visit to South Asia*

She's not a dog, but I—you know—she's not gorgeous. I'd give her a five.

> Representative STEVE CHABOT (R–Ohio) in 1995, responding to the question, "Do you think Hillary Clinton is pretty?" put to him by a Spy magazine interviewer posing as a reporter for the fictitious publication Republican Beat: The GOP Magazine for Teens

I think she's attractive. . . . She has big hips but I can't say that.

> Representative ROBERT NEY (R–Ohio) in 1995, responding to Spy's Hillary query, for which he later apologized in a letter to Mrs. Clinton

Powers Behind the Throne: Political Spouses

Oh, boo. Women have been facing the harshest realities of life since the beginning of time.

> ELIZABETH TAYLOR, interrupting a speech by husband No. 6, John Warner, during his first race for a Virginia senate seat, objecting to his assertion that women don't belong in combat because it is the harshest reality of modern existence

We became Vice President.

> BARBARA BUSH's characteristic expression for describing her family's new job after the election victory of the Reagan-Bush ticket in 1980

Who needs this debate? Let's go out and party!

> GEORGETTE MOSBACHER, *wife of GOP fund-raising chief Robert*
> *Mosbacher, in 1992, joking to Judy Black, wife of GOP strategist*
> *Charles Black, at the third presidential debate*

Which two are you?

> BARBARA BUSH *in 1992, to New York Post columnist William*
> *Norwich, who had said the Bush campaign denigrates women, Jewish*
> *intellectuals, and gays, adding that he fits into two of the groups. In*
> *reply, Norwich said, "All three, ma'am, on a Saturday night."*

I'm outta here.

> BARBARA BUSH *in 1992, after tiring of photo-ops while campaigning*
> *at an Illinois grade school*

It means you'd throw yourself on a live hand grenade for George Bush.
I'm not sure Millie would, but I think she would. But I know I would
because I know he'd do the same for us. . . . Millie said in her book—I
think it would be Millie, not I, who'd make this brilliant statement—
that you have to adore someone who adores you.

> BARBARA BUSH *in 1992, asked to explain the dedication, "To George*
> *Bush, whom we both love more than life" in Millie's Book, the*
> *bestseller coauthored by the First Lady and the First Pet*

Absolute pure animal magnetism. Suddenly there was just the two of
us. Everyone else just melted away.

> TIPPER GORE *in 1993, on her impression of Al Gore when they*
> *first met*

Yuck.

> Wendy Lee Gramm, *on her impression of husband, Senator Phil Gramm, when they first met. Gramm, then a professor at Texas A&M who was recruiting new teachers at the time, introduced himself by saying that Texas A&M could use a pretty instructor like her on its faculty.*

You'd have to ask her that.

> Dan Quayle *in 1993, to reporters who asked if "a Quayle" was thinking of running for governor of Indiana*

Now how did a couple of nice old ladies like us get involved in a mess like this?

> Georgie Packwood *in 1993, to Penny Durenberger, referring to the ethics-related questions dogging their husbands, Senators Bob Packwood and Dave Durenberger*

───────── **Reality Check** ─────────

Behind every successful man is a surprised woman.

> Maryon Pearson, *wife of Canadian prime minister Lester Pearson*

───────────── ◆ ─────────────

Dutifully walk three paces behind her. Drive the car. And keep your mouth shut.

> Tony Morella, *husband of Representative Constance Morella (R–Md.), in 1995, offering spousal conduct tips to newcomer Ed Kelly, husband of Representative Sue Kelly (R–N.Y.)*

Pray for me. Don't brag. And don't talk to Connie Chung.
BARBARA BUSH *in 1995, on what son and Texas governor George W. Bush asks of her*

She is what we want our mom to be like.
Outlaw Biker *magazine publisher* CASEY EXTON *in 1995, on choosing Barbara Bush over Hillary Rodham Clinton as "The First Lady of the Century"*

If I want to knock a story off the front page, I just change my hairstyle.
HILLARY RODHAM CLINTON *in 1995, on her strategy for counteracting negative press coverage*

I never said anything about loafers.
HILLARY RODHAM CLINTON *in 1995, on a* Washington Times *report that said the First Lady dictates everything from her husband's shoe style (laces, not loafers) to the overexposure of the chief executive's thighs while he's jogging (she insists he wear long pants)*

He'd much rather have me delivering his speeches than to be in Bill Clinton's shoes and have Hillary Clinton write them.
GAYLE WILSON, *wife of California governor Pete Wilson, in 1995. Mrs. Wilson delivered her husband's first 1996 presidential campaign speech, since he was recovering from surgery that kept him from using his vocal chords.*

Watching Hillary has just been a horrible experience. Hillary sticking her neck out is not working.

MARIANNE GINGRICH, *wife of House speaker Newt Gingrich, in 1995, sympathizing with the First Lady and expressing doubts that she could ever enjoy the job*

•5•

The Bobster: Mr. Dole Goes to Washington

Live it up while you can, Mary Rose. We're parked in a ten-minute zone.

> *Newly elected congressman* BOB DOLE *at a 1961 White House reception held by President John Kennedy to honor the freshmen in Congress, responding to the wife of a fellow freshman, who, caught up in the glamour of the event, had gushed, "Oh Bob, isn't it perfect?"*

Finally made it. Lots of Democrats here.

> *Freshman congressman* BOB DOLE *in an inscription on a photograph of himself on the Capitol steps that he sent home to Kansas at the beginning of his first stint in Washington. At the time, in the early 1960s, Democrats controlled the White House and both houses of Congress.*

I went to visit Disneyland and found Mickey Mouse
wearing a Spiro Agnew watch.

Freshman senator BOB DOLE *in 1969, an early doubter
of his own party's recently elected vice president, who
would resign from office in 1973 due to ethics violations.
At the unveiling of an Agnew bust on Capitol Hill in
1995, a kinder, gentler Dole praised Agnew, saying of his
support of America's involvement in Vietnam, "Millions
of Americans were proud to stand with him."*

──────────── ♦ ────────────

Musta been my night off.

BOB DOLE, *national chairman of the Republican National
Committee, when asked in the mid-1970s about the RNC's possible
role in the White House bugging operation at the Democratic National
Committee's offices in Washington, D.C.'s, Watergate office-
apartment complex, the building in which Dole himself eventually
made his residence*

Well, we got the burglar vote.

BOB DOLE, *chairman of the RNC, in 1973, when asked how
revelations about the Watergate break-in would affect GOP fortunes
in the next election*

I think Ford's given me about all the help I can stand.

BOB DOLE *in 1974, asked if he was anticipating the assistance of President Gerald Ford in the upcoming elections, in which Dole would nearly lose his own Senate seat. Dole's reference was to Ford's unpopular pardon of Richard Nixon for any crimes committed in connection with the Watergate scandal.*

Did you put in a *burial allowance,* for the ones who will *starve?*

BOB DOLE *to fellow senator James Buckley in 1975, opposing Buckley's proposed bill to discourage poor people from collecting food stamps*

I used to call him southern-fried McGovern . . . but I have a lot of respect for Senator McGovern.

BOB DOLE *in 1976, on Democratic presidential candidate Jimmy Carter. Dole amended the description on being advised that it might offend Southern voters. Dole, who ridiculed Democratic presidential nominee McGovern in 1972, had indeed grown to like the South Dakota senator, having cosponsored a 1975 bill with him that would have made food stamps easier to collect.*

They told me to go for the jugular—so I did. It was mine.

A rueful BOB DOLE *in the aftermath of the 1976 defeat of the Ford-Dole ticket, on his role as designated scrapper in the GOP campaign*

There they are—See No Evil, Hear No Evil, and Evil.
> BOB DOLE *on a gathering of former presidents*
> *Gerald Ford, Jimmy Carter, and Richard Nixon*

————————— ♦ —————————

Good news is, a bus full of supply-siders went over a cliff last night. . . .
Bad news is, there were three empty seats.
> BOB DOLE *on President Ronald Reagan's economic advisers, who*
> *promoted a policy of using a tax-cut-induced jump in consumer*
> *spending to reduce the federal deficit rather than Dole's preferred*
> *method of cuts in defense and other government spending*

But I think right now they ought to circle the wagons—either that, or
let a couple of wagons go over the cliff.
> BOB DOLE *in the mid-1980s, saying that while he would never advise*
> *President Reagan to fire his chief of staff or secretary of state over the*
> *bungled handling of the Iran-contra revelations, he did have to wonder*
> *why those two individuals were so unequal to the task of defending*
> *the president*

Don't think Ripley'd believe that.
> BOB DOLE *in the mid-1980s, on the Reagan administration's*
> *insistence that only two relatively minor White House officials were*
> *"in the loop" about the Iran-contra arms-for-hostages deal*

He not only brings home the bacon, he brings home the whole hog!

> Bob Dole, *usually a reliable critic of government spending, heaping praise on the pork-barrel prowess of Senator Mark Andrews of North Dakota, on whose behalf he campaigned in 1986*

He's making a lot of noise but I don't see any impact.

> Bob Dole *in the mid-1980s, on a rising star in Congress named Newt Gingrich*

Walked into the cloakroom [of the Senate] the other day, and yelled, "Mr. President!" Twenty guys turned around!

> Bob Dole *in 1986, on the burgeoning field of GOP presidential nominee wannabe's*

First thing that guy ought to do is get a shave. . . .

> Bob Dole *in 1987 on the controversy over Reagan Supreme Court nominee Robert Bork, whose appointment Dole supported in vain. The bearded professor, conservative judicial opinions notwithstanding, had the physical appearance of an aging hippie.*

Well, at least you'll remember the introduction.

> Bob Dole *at a 1987 fund-raiser, somewhat dazed after his wife, Elizabeth Hanford Dole, had introduced him as a war hero who spent 39 months in the hospital recovering from his wounds and endured eight operations . . . an aspect of his private life that Dole had always suppressed*

They thought I could get elected because I'd been shot.

> BOB DOLE *in 1987, campaigning for the presidency, telling a Michigan audience about how his political career began in 1950, when leaders of the local Republican and Democratic parties both visited the Second World War veteran who had lost the use of one arm during combat, urging him to run for the legislature. Dole said he picked the GOP because they held a 2-to-1 registration advantage in his native Russell County, Kansas.*

You know, I have a feeling I'm not going to make much news today.

> BOB DOLE *in 1987, sharing a platform at a convention of media executives with Gary Hart at the moment when revelations broke concerning Hart's rumored paramour Donna Rice*

I guess I wouldn't go to the *mountaintop*, come back with a *vision*, you know. . . .

> *Presidential candidate* BOB DOLE, *who was suspicious of visions and of people motivated by Big Ideas, in 1987, explaining to a friend why a potential campaign guru had spurned Dole's invitation to help out with his presidential bid*

Hey! We got vision! We even got vision music!

> BOB DOLE *in 1988, boarding his campaign plane to the strains of the* Star Wars *soundtrack*

You know, I'm not running again. Sometimes you have to lose, and it makes you stronger. You can come back. But I'm not running again. This is my time.

> BOB DOLE, *who lost a previous bid for the presidency in 1980, during his 1988 bid for the presidency—seven years prior to his next bid for the presidency*

Of course, you could say I was from Texas. I was stationed at Camp Barkley, near Abilene, in the war. . . . I got to Texas before George Bush!

> BOB DOLE *in 1988, on his rival for the GOP presidential nomination, George Bush, who was born in Massachusetts, raised in Greenwich, Connecticut, made his oil fortune in Texas, summered at the family compound in Kennebunkport, Maine—a candidate from everywhere and from nowhere, it seemed to Dole*

Stop lying about my record!

> BOB DOLE *in 1988, attacking rival GOP presidential candidate George Bush on the night of Dole's defeat at Bush's hands in the New Hampshire primary*

Give it to George. I'd have to read it first.

> BOB DOLE *in a televised 1988 debate among contenders for the Republican presidential nomination prior to the New Hampshire primary, responding to rival Pete du Pont's suggestion that he sign a copy of the traditional New Hampshire no-tax pledge by implying that George Bush might be game, but he wasn't*

He just—the elevator doors opened and there he was, with just one guy, frail, alone. . . . You know, suddenly, I *believed* he had to push that girl off his lap.

> Bob Dole *in 1988, on an encounter with fellow senator Gary Hart on Capitol Hill. Describing in 1987 an early encounter with Donna Rice, Hart had said, "This attractive lady whom I had only recently been introduced to dropped into my lap. . . . I chose not to dump her off."*

They ought to calm down, go out for a weekend, have a diet Coke, enjoy yourself.

> Bob Dole *in 1993, joking that the Clinton administration acted as if an election campaign was still on. Clinton political adviser George Stephanopoulos replied, "I don't know if I'd agree with that, but it's very thoughtful advice."*

Our intent will not be to create gridlock. Oh, except maybe from time to time.

> Bob Dole *in 1993, on prospects for bipartisan dealings with the new Clinton administration*

Gridlock? Pork-lock, pork-lock.

> Bob Dole *in 1993, defending the GOP filibuster that held up the Clinton administration's $16 billion jobs bill*

Before I got this honorary doctorate, Senator Mitchell called me "Mr. Gridlock." But with this degree, I will insist on being called "Dr. Gridlock."

> BOB DOLE *in 1993, after being honored by Colby College in Maine*

Life is very important to Americans.

> BOB DOLE *in 1994, asked on a C-Span program whether U.S. lives are more valuable than foreign ones*

Every time I look at Strom Thurmond, I'm inspired. . . . When I see him eat a banana, I eat a banana.

> BOB DOLE *in 1994, claiming he wouldn't be too old for a presidential run in 1996, when he will be 73. Senator Thurmond (R–S.C.) was 92 at the time.*

I thought it was, particularly if she had known I'd had prostate cancer.

> BOB DOLE *in 1994, asked whether he thought Oscar-night host Whoopi Goldberg's joke about him—"Bob Dole, meet Lorena Bobbitt"—was in bad taste. Bobbitt was convicted of amputating her husband's penis.*

I was a bit surprised. Maybe my endorsement of him caused him to withdraw.

> BOB DOLE *in 1994, on Senator George Mitchell's decision to remove himself from consideration for appointment to the Supreme Court*

It's not too popular. I can already see, when you start cutting programs that might affect low-income Americans, it might become an issue. The public senses that $4.5 million is a lot of money.

BOB DOLE *in 1994, expressing his misgivings about the contrast between Newt Gingrich's message of austerity in government and his recently signed $4.5 million contract to write his memoirs*

---------------- **Reality Check** ----------------

You can go out there and say, "I've got nine ideas." Well, maybe one of them is good. We're the party of ideas, but that doesn't mean every idea is a good idea. You hear Gingrich's staff has these five file cabinets, four big ones and one little tiny one. No. 1 is "Newt's Ideas," No. 2, "Newt's Ideas," No. 3, No. 4, "Newt's Ideas." The little one is "Newt's Good Ideas."

BOB DOLE *in 1995, countering the criticism that he lacks vision by suggesting that his House counterpart Gingrich is perhaps overly blessed with it*

------------------- ♦ -------------------

At least she's president of something, which is more than I can say.

BOB DOLE *in 1995, on his wife, Elizabeth, who is head of the Red Cross*

Brother, you don't know the half of it. The only reason Elizabeth was helping was because they were taking pictures.

    Bob Dole *responding to a letter from a Californian who was irate on seeing a photograph in* People *magazine of Washington power couple Bob and Elizabeth Hanford Dole making their bed. "Senator, you're causing problems for men all over the country," the correspondent wrote. "Ever since that picture, I have to help my wife make the bed."*

You know how old this elephant is? Forty-eight—a young Republican!

    Bob Dole *in 1995, accepting a photo-op with King Tusk, an elephant from a circus visiting Capitol Hill*

Hope you sleep better this year. Ought to, with Republicans in charge.

    Bob Dole *in 1995, greeting the staff of the "Today" show on the first day of the GOP-controlled 104th Congress*

Agghh, my mother would have said, "Off the record."

    Bob Dole *in 1995, on Kathleen Gingrich's indiscreet disclosure to Connie Chung of her son's uncharitable assessment of Hillary Rodham Clinton*

He's in the right wing of the Capitol. But to get there you gotta take a right, then you take another far right, and then you go to the extreme right, and he should be right there.

    Bob Dole *in 1995, offering to help the "Tonight" show staff track down the office of freshman congressman Sonny Bono (R–Calif.)*

——————— Reality Check ———————

I didn't want him running out in the street scaring people.
BOB DOLE *in 1995, saying he had given Bill Clinton*
$250 toward construction of a White House jogging track

————————— ♦ —————————

Stop paying Clinton speechwriters by the word. Arkansas? Sell it.
BOB DOLE *in a 1995 appearance on* Late Night With David
Letterman, *the unusual forum he chose for announcing that he would
seek the GOP presidential nomination in 1996. Dole brought a "Top
7" list of ways to cut the budget. Asked why he hadn't brought the
traditional "Top 10" list, Dole explained that "Republicans are cutting
everything by 30%."*

Reining in government and all that other stuff.
BOB DOLE *in 1995, outlining his detailed presidential
campaign platform*

Lamar's out there every day claiming he's the outsider. I remember
meeting him when *I* came to Washington.
BOB DOLE *in 1995, on GOP presidential nomination rival Lamar
Alexander's bid to position himself as a Washington outsider. Dole by
that point had served in Congress for 34 years.*

──── Reality Check ────

We've never had a president named Bob. And I think
it's time.

> BOB DOLE *in April 1995, announcing his*
> *presidential candidacy*

──────── ◆ ────────

I was conservative before he was out of high school.

> BOB DOLE, *71, responding to the comment of 52-year-old*
> *Phil Gramm when making his own declaration to seek the presidency*
> *that he was conservative before it was fashionable*

Everybody says the most dangerous place in the Capitol is between Phil and a TV camera.

> BOB DOLE *in 1995, on publicity hound and GOP presidential rival*
> *Phil Gramm*

I remember a couple, maybe three, years ago, he started introducing me as the best legislator he'd ever known. . . . All this fulsome praise about Bob Dole, the greatest Senator in the world. In other words, he oughtta stay there. I thought, "This guy is running for President!" Three years ago! I couldn't believe it.

> BOB DOLE *in 1995, on Phil Gramm's early ambitions*

I was sort of the lightning rod. I finally got a little relief this year. . . . Everywhere, people go, "This is the *nice* Bob Dole, the voice of reason."

> BOB DOLE *in 1995, insisting he is pleased to be in the shadow of the*
> *new House Speaker, Newt Gingrich*

---------------- **Reality Check** ----------------

I listen to all these politicians. They were all born in a log cabin. Give me a break.

> BOB DOLE *in 1995, on his lifelong reluctance to use his*
> *personal history of Depression-era deprivation and*
> *permanent injuries sustained as a decorated war veteran*
> *as a means of winning votes*

---------------- ♦ ----------------

I don't think I'm mean. . . . I don't throw things at my wife or the staff.
BOB DOLE, *long known as the "Republican hatchet man" for his role in the 1976 presidential campaign as Gerald Ford's running mate, in 1995, on his new, more mellow mood. The reference is to rumors that Bill and Hillary Rodham Clinton toss things at each other during White House arguments.*

But I was smiling when I said it.
BOB DOLE *in a "Meet the Press" appearance a few days after declaring his presidential candidacy in April 1995, when his comment that things will be different "when we have a real president in the Oval Office" prompted the show's host to remark, "This doesn't sound like the kinder, friendlier 'new Bob Dole' "*

Yes, we have an obligation to help those who need us. I remember as county attorney in Russell County, Kansas, signing welfare checks for my grandparents, who were caught up in the dust bowl days.
Welfare-reform proponent BOB DOLE *in 1995, acknowledging the virtues of welfare. Actually, Dole was county attorney from 1952 to 1960, not in the dust-bowl 1930s.*

If you really feel patriotic today, she'll take your blood.
BOB DOLE *at a 1995 New Hampshire presidential campaign appearance, referring to his wife, Elizabeth, head of the American Red Cross*

My cholesterol's lower than Clinton's, my blood pressure's lower than Clinton's, my weight is less than Clinton's. I am not going to make health an issue.

> BOB DOLE, 72, in 1995, on the age factor in the 1996 presidential race. Bill Clinton responded, "[My pulse rate] is much lower than Dole's, but . . . I don't have to deal with Phil Gramm every day."

People are more interested in a strong economy than someone who can tell you if Hootie & the Blowfish are going to have a strong album next time.

> Dole press secretary NELSON WARFIELD in 1995, on why being hip won't be an issue for candidates in the 1996 presidential contest

I'm willing to be another Ronald Reagan if that's what you want.

> BOB DOLE in 1995, to a group of prominent GOP members

·6·

The Ides of Newt

Newtisms

The American Army could not last a weekend in Western Europe against the Russians. The Sixth Fleet could not last a full day against the Soviet fleet.

NEWT GINGRICH *in a 1974 campaign position paper*

You do not want to elect politicians who say "Trust me," 'cause you can't trust anybody.

NEWT GINGRICH *in a 1978 speech to College Republicans*

"Gunsmoke" normally had very little violence, it was really sort of a soap opera with cowboys and people sat around the saloon and talked with Kitty, and "Doc" dropped by. . . . The show did not begin with 12 people gang-raping Kitty, or the marshal saying, "Gee, we cannot get involved, the ACLU will get upset."

NEWT GINGRICH *in a 1984 Congressional address*

Show me a wagon train that has food stamps.

> NEWT GINGRICH *in 1984, responding to Mario Cuomo's rousing indictment of Reagan-era poverty at the Democratic National Convention*

I heard a radio report that Jodie Foster had been found with cocaine coming [into] the United States, but there was "insufficient quantity to arrest her. . . ." Now . . . what if I described to you a nation in which a cocaine user would be let go, but seven parents who wanted to send their children to a school so they could learn about God would be arrested. That would sound like the Soviet Union, like Nazi Germany, or a degenerate dictatorship.

> NEWT GINGRICH *in a 1984 Congressional address*

The ACLU . . . verges on paranoia, is almost psychopathic in its commitment to a vision of an American danger that simply does not exist, that is literally impossible except in the most esoteric salons of the liberal elite of this country.

> NEWT GINGRICH *in 1984, on the American Civil Liberties Union*

It is essential to understand why *The Killing Fields* had rave reviews from left-wing intellectuals, while *Rambo* was laughed at. *Rambo* was overtly anti-Communist, while *The Killing Fields* managed to somehow pin the blame on America for what was clearly a Communist genocidal action in Cambodia.

> NEWT GINGRICH *in a 1986 Congressional address*

The welfare state kills more poor people in a year than private business.

NEWT GINGRICH *in 1989*

The idea that a congressman would be tainted by accepting money from private industry or private sources is essentially a socialist argument.

NEWT GINGRICH *in 1989, on accepting campaign funds from*
lobbyists and other special interests

That was no bimbo. That was my wife.

NEWT GINGRICH *in 1989, on hearing that a newspaper had published*
a story about him kissing a "bimbo" on a Washington street

The words *and* phrases are powerful. Read them. Memorize as many as possible. And remember that, like any tool, these words will not help if they are not used.

Introduction to Language, a Key Mechanism of Control, *a*
guidebook distributed to Republican candidates and prepared by
GOPAC, a political action committee of which Newt Gingrich was
general chairman when the fall 1990 distribution was made. Among
the "Optimistic Positive Governing Words" to be used by Republican
candidates in description of themselves were "truth, courage,
prosperity, humane, pristine, liberty, dream, strength." Among the
"Contrasting Words" with which to "define our opponents" were
"decay, failure, collapse, destructive, destroy, sick, pathetic, betray,
coercion, traitors, hypocrisy, devour, waste, corruption, incompetent,
permissive, bizarre, self-serving, greed, stagnation, taxes, shame,
disgrace, lie, cheat, steal."

Mussolini, Stalin and Hitler would have admired some of the elite campuses where certain words can get a student expelled.

NEWT GINGRICH *in 1991, on political correctness*

In this city, if you are the conservative spokesman, you're going to get your brains blown out.

NEWT GINGRICH *in 1991, on life in Washington, D.C.*

This [the 1992 Congressional campaign] is the most miserable campaign I've ever been in. I've seriously considered just quitting, just saying, "This filth is so sickening, I don't want to be part of it anymore."

NEWT GINGRICH *in 1992, responding to charges by the Democratic opponent in his Georgia Congressional district, Tony Center, who ran advertisements about the details of the breakup of Gingrich's first marriage*

I mean, one of the things we know historically, biologically, is that males are designed to be relatively irresponsible and every healthy society on the planet tries to maximize male responsibility.

NEWT GINGRICH *in 1992*

All healthy societies understand that one of their primary goals is to train, educate, and acculturate young males. The young males are the most dangerous physically, and they're the most dangerous in terms of being totally irresponsible. Because they are driven biologically to be nomadic, and to leave as many pregnant women behind as they can. And that's a biological reality.

NEWT GINGRICH *in a 1992 speech to Young Republicans*

Well, as the photographer in my family, I'm the one who shoots the giraffes.

> TIPPER GORE, *wife of Vice President Al Gore, in 1995, responding to Newt Gingrich's suggestion that men are better at combat because "males are biologically driven to go out and hunt giraffes"*

♦

You cannot get to universal coverage without a police state.

> NEWT GINGRICH *in 1994, opposing Bill Clinton's health-care reform agenda*

Why should a $20,000-a-year worker with two children have their taxes transferred to Frank Sinatra and David Rockefeller to pay for the Medicare premiums?

> NEWT GINGRICH *in 1993*

It's a devastating issue if you're on the wrong side of it.

> NEWT GINGRICH *in 1994, on ethics*

I was dramatically shaped by my grandmother and my aunts because they convinced me there was always a cookie available. Deep down inside me I'm four years old, and I wake up and I think out there, there's a cookie. Every morning I'm going, you know, either it can be baked or it's already been bought, but it's in a jar . . . somewhere. . . .

And so that means when you open up the cupboard and the cookie isn't there, I don't say, "Gee, there's no cookie." I say, "I wonder where it is."

NEWT GINGRICH *in 1994, in the Renewing American Civilization lecture series*

We are looking for a dacha. We think Leon and George need dachas.
> NEWT GINGRICH, *recommending retirement for White House chief of staff Leon Panetta and presidential adviser George Stephanopoulos*

I personally favor mandatory requirement of work for everybody, including women with young children.
> NEWT GINGRICH, *in the Renewing American Civilization lecture series*

It's the pursuit of happiness. There are no happiness stamps, there is no federal department of happiness. Each individual has to be engaged in the pursuit, not guaranteed the finding.
> NEWT GINGRICH *in 1994, interpreting the Declaration of Independence*

[There should be] a way for decent people to run for office without being so humiliated and so scarred up.
> NEWT GINGRICH *on election night 1994, appealing for civility in politics*

The mother killing the two children in South Carolina vividly reminds every American how sick the society is getting and how much we need to change things. The only way you get change is to vote Republican.
> NEWT GINGRICH *in November 1994, suggesting that Susan Smith, charged with murdering her two children, was motivated by a climate of liberal permissiveness—a comment that drew charges that Gingrich was attempting to exploit the tragedy to generate votes*

I understand my critics are fixated and pathologically disoriented, but they are my opponents. Why would I try to correct them?

NEWT GINGRICH *in 1994*

———————————— ♦ ————————————

Politics and war are remarkably similar situations.

NEWT GINGRICH *in 1995, on his philosophy that politics is a winner-take-all fight, whose import is similar to war in its effect on the lives of ordinary people*

In the 19th century, no major figure served more than 12 years in the House.

NEWT GINGRICH, *congressman and former assistant professor of history at tiny West Georgia State College, in 1994, arguing in favor of term limits. In fact, 103 members served more than 12 consecutive years in the House of Representatives in the last century.*

I think it's perfectly legitimate in a free society for people to decide where they'll put their money and their impact.

House Speaker NEWT GINGRICH *in 1995, suggesting that advertisers should not do business with the many newspaper editorial boards that have "socialists" on them and that draft "editorials that only make sense if people believe that government's good and the free market is bad. Surely you can't really argue that there aren't a substantial number of news editorial pages that start from an extraordinarily pro-government, anti-free-market bias."*

We're maintaining a fabric of education within which they can pursue their social life. This is crazy.

> NEWT GINGRICH *in 1995, saying that high school should be reduced to two or three years because government shouldn't be in the business of "subsidizing dating"*

You either have a system where you say, "Would you like to learn how to be rich, would you like to learn how to be successful?" Or you have a system where you say, "Well, you really ought to feel envy and resentment, so let's see if we can mug them."

> NEWT GINGRICH *in 1995, proposing cuts to the Public Broadcasting Service*

Princeton sent me a rejection letter so elegantly worded that I still think of myself as an alumna.

> NEWT GINGRICH *in 1995. Gingrich, who failed in his first two bids for a Congressional seat and embarked on his third, and successful, attempt after being told he would not be granted tenure at West Georgia State College, speaks to his lingering animus toward Princeton University for turning down his application to become a doctoral student at the Ivy League institution.*

We are a happy band of Vikings, who don't mind a fight!

> NEWT GINGRICH *in January 1995, during the effort to pass legislation in the first 100 days of his party's "Contract With America" legislative program*

[It's] Washington at its most bizarre.

NEWT GINGRICH *in 1995, on being lobbied by his lesbian half-sister about gay rights. Gingrich's mother, Kathleen, said of her daughter, "I accept Candy. . . . But I do wish that Candy would be—how should I say it?—natural."*

Notice how small and unprepossessing they are?

NEWT GINGRICH, *admiring a fire-belly newt brought to his office by a visitor from Washington's National Zoo*

I'm going to look for moose and butterflies.

NEWT GINGRICH *in 1995, insisting on an innocent motive behind an upcoming trip to New Hampshire—traditionally a required first step on the road to the presidency. Gingrich's remark was a coy reminder to reporters that John Kennedy went to New Hampshire saying he was only going there to "hunt moose," and that Thomas Jefferson, enroute to New York State to found the Democratic Party, insisted that his motive was only to "collect butterflies." Remarking on the historical company Gingrich likes to keep, columnist Paul Gigot of The Wall Street Journal noted that "Gingrich's ego is now so large that he doesn't compare himself to just a single world-historical figure when two are available."*

My fear is that Oliver Stone would remake it as a film about cannibalism in an orphanage.

NEWT GINGRICH *in 1995, asked if Hollywood should remake the film* Boys Town

If the Soviet empire still existed, I'd be terrified. The fact is, we can afford a fairly ignorant presidency now.

NEWT GINGRICH in 1989

──────────────── ♦ ────────────────

The Last Couch Potato.

NEWT GINGRICH in 1995, telling actor and fitness buff Arnold
Schwarzenegger the name of the film he'd soon be starring in if he
didn't start exercising

I would really love to spend six months to a year in the Amazon basin, just being able to spend the day watching tree sloths.

NEWT GINGRICH in 1995

As a person I have a particular affection for rhinos.

NEWT GINGRICH in a 1995 House speech, coming to the defense of a
tiny federal program slated to be cut—$800,000 to help African and
Asian nations preserve the rhinoceros, the tiger, and the elephant—
during a Congressional session in which Gingrich's GOP majority
reduced foreign aid spending by several million dollars, and cut $9.3
billion from domestic human welfare programs in education, labor,
and health care. "Don't allow them to disappear," Gingrich
successfully pleaded on behalf of the exotic animals, "and join the
dinosaur skull in my office."

The only money goes to the kids. So if you have $1,000, you can pay . . . for 500 books, whereas in the welfare state model, if you have $1,000, you pay $850 of it for the bureaucracy.

NEWT GINGRICH in a January 21, 1995, televised lecture, promoting his "Earning by Learning" scheme, which pays schoolchildren $2 for every book they read. On July 17, 1995, The Wall Street Journal reported that Mel Steely, a history professor at West Georgia College who is writing Gingrich's authorized biography and runs the EBL program at the college, collected fees that totaled nearly half of the scheme's $62,000 endowment.

In the broad sense I am a teacher. I start out thinking about civilization [with a] holistic or Gestalt kind of approach [and the motto] "Listen, learn, help, and lead."

NEWT GINGRICH in 1995, allowing that his pedagogical influences of the moment range from Arnold Toynbee to Isaac Asimov

I don't do foreign policy.

NEWT GINGRICH in 1995, when asked if he had thought about leading a delegation to China to repair troubled relations between China and the U.S.

Talking is more tiring than I thought.

NEWT GINGRICH in 1995, wrapping up his 25-city tour promoting his book To Renew America

A Man with a Mission

[My ambition] is to be an old-time political boss in 20 years.
> NEWT GINGRICH *in 1974, recalling his days as an organizer of the*
> *Young Republicans at Emory University in the 1960s*

─────────── Reality Check ───────────

I have an enormous personal ambition. I want to shift the
entire planet. And I'm doing it. I am now a famous
person. . . . I represent real power.
> NEWT GINGRICH *in 1985*

─────────── ♦ ───────────

If you decide in your freshman year in high school that your job is to
spend your lifetime trying to change the future of your people, you're
probably fairly weird. I think I was pretty weird as a kid.
> NEWT GINGRICH *in 1985*

I'm willing to say, having gone through the last five and six years and
having understood that—as an incorrigible bulldozer—it's conceivable
I was that insensitive. It was never in any sense deliberate.
> NEWT GINGRICH *in 1989, commenting on the story that he asked for*
> *a divorce while his first wife Jackie Battley was recovering*
> *from surgery*

People like me are what stand between us and Auschwitz. I see evil around me every day.

NEWT GINGRICH *in 1994*

Reality Check

Every reform movement has a lunatic fringe.

THEODORE ROOSEVELT *in 1913*

I am a revolutionary centrist.

NEWT GINGRICH

Conservative futurist.

NEWT GINGRICH'S *paradoxical self-description*

I will not rest until I have transformed the landscape of American politics.

NEWT GINGRICH *in 1991*

My uncle taught me to smile at Eisenhower on the television and to turn Adlai Stevenson off.

NEWT GINGRICH *in 1994*

Renew American civilization [and] redirect the fate of the human race.

NEWT GINGRICH *in 1994, on his career goal*

Power corrupts, but lack of power corrupts absolutely.

ADLAI STEVENSON

————————————— ♦ —————————————

It just seems to me it all boils down to leadership. Not that I'm such a great leader. But I think I'm at least an inch or two above the others. And that's going to be our message.

NEWT GINGRICH

What is the primary purpose of a political leader? To build a majority. If [voters] care about parking lots, then talk about parking lots.

NEWT GINGRICH, *explaining that issues of the day should not be treated too seriously for their own sake, but mostly as a means of consolidating power*

Certainly a name like Newt Gingrich is weird enough that it sort of fits the classic American pattern. Maybe there's a long tradition in America with people with unusual backgrounds having an opportunity to rise.

NEWT GINGRICH *in 1994*

If I were to act as Speaker the way I acted as minority whip, I would be an idiot—and we would fail. When I was the minority whip, I could say virtually anything, because it wasn't going to happen.

Incoming House Speaker NEWT GINGRICH *in 1994, following a conciliatory meeting with President Bill Clinton and incoming Senate majority leader Bob Dole*

Because I am now the next Speaker, I am learning that everything I say has to be worded carefully and thought through at a level that I've never experienced in my life.

NEWT GINGRICH in 1994

You grow up an army brat named Newton and you learn about combat.

NEWT GINGRICH in 1995

American Gaullist.

NEWT GINGRICH in 1995, when asked to suggest a label that best describes him. Among Gingrich's heroes is French president Charles de Gaulle, who united the country in the aftermath of World War II.

How would you use who I am becoming?

NEWT GINGRICH in 1995, to his advisers after a speech to a group of admirers

On the Clintons

What you got was Dukakis with a Southern accent.

NEWT GINGRICH on the similarities between Bill Clinton and the 1988 Democratic presidential nominee Michael Dukakis

[To compare Bush and Clinton] the line I've been using is that to decide you're irritated with Bush on taxes and decide to marry Clinton is like having dated a social drinker and ended up marrying a bartender. Bush may have some weaknesses on the tax side, but compared to Clinton he's almost—you know.

NEWT GINGRICH *in 1992*

Reality Check

[Clinton would] be a good guy to have a beer with. He'd be a great frat president.

NEWT GINGRICH *in 1994*

We were thinking, this is good. You know, this is like watching the President get into his Mustang and drive straight into a ditch. You say, "Oh, look at that!"

NEWT GINGRICH *in 1994, on the temporary stall in Congress of President Clinton's crime bill*

There's a part of him that's just automatically compassionate with anybody. It's transactional, it has no policy meaning.

NEWT GINGRICH *in 1994, on President Bill Clinton*

You have to love people enough to want to change them, not just feel their pain.

NEWT GINGRICH *in 1995, in direct reference to* Boys Town *and indirectly to Bill Clinton*

When I hear a Clinton speech, I'm normally applauding and saying, "Boy, I agree with that."

NEWT GINGRICH *in 1995, on Bill Clinton*

On the Democrats

The pompous politicians who lead this majority party [the Democrats] are the Pharisees. They stand in the doorway refusing to enter themselves, but blocking the pathway of anyone else who might wish to.

NEWT GINGRICH *in 1975*

In 1960 I worked very hard in Columbus [Georgia] for the Nixon/ Lodge ticket. One of the longest nights of my life was that election when, as a high school senior, I listened on radio to the Chicago and Texas machines stealing the election. That bitter pill became even more bitter 14 years later when the people who had profited from their own theft in 1960 became pious and served as judges in Congress on the man they had stolen from.

NEWT GINGRICH *in 1976*

In my lifetime, without question, the president who lied the most and did the most damage to the United States was Lyndon Johnson. It was Johnson who misled the American people about war in Asia. It was Johnson who designed a disastrous economic policy that fueled the inflation from which we are only now recovering. It was Johnson's politics of irresponsible promises which led to riots on the campuses and in the cities. It is Johnson's "Great Society" which is smothering us in red tape, fiscal deficits, and massive bureaucracy.

NEWT GINGRICH *in 1976*

If you like welfare cheaters, you'll love Virginia Shapard.

Flyer for Newt Gingrich's 1978 Congressional campaign, noting that local Democrats Shapard and black civil-rights leader Julian Bond opposed a welfare reform bill

I think, based on the historical record, he is the most unethical Speaker of the 20th century.

NEWT GINGRICH *in 1987, on Jim Wright*

This man is so despicable and so desperate to be a congressman that he is deliberately scaring 80- and 90-year-old people with what he knows is a lie.

NEWT GINGRICH *in 1988, referring to opponent Dennis Worley's charges that Gingrich aimed to eradicate Social Security*

The reports I've seen indicate that his wife [Kitty Dukakis] was a drug addict for 27 years, on diet pills. Dukakis's answer when asked about it was, he had not noticed.

NEWT GINGRICH *in July 1988, campaigning against the Democratic presidential ticket headed by Michael Dukakis*

[Democrats] have rigged the game better than Noriega. . . . The fact is, in almost any other business in America we spend vastly more money trying to communicate with the American people than we do in campaigns. Look at the cost of advertising beer.

NEWT GINGRICH *in 1989, referring to Democratic criticism of Republican campaign spending "excesses" and the rigged elections of Panamanian dictator Manuel Noriega*

They [Georgia Democratic Party leaders] are pleasant people who behind the scenes are thugs.

NEWT GINGRICH *in 1989*

A trio of muggers.
> NEWT GINGRICH's *label in 1989 for Democratic House leaders Jim Wright, Tip O'Neill, and Tom Foley*

A left-wing lynch mob.
> NEWT GINGRICH *in 1989, on the Democrats leading the Congressional inquiry into the Iran-contra scandal*

Pro-communist.
> NEWT GINGRICH's *label in 1989 for Democratic House Speaker Jim Wright during Wright's efforts to negotiate with the Sandanista-led government of Nicaragua*

As a human I've always felt sympathy for him [Jim Wright]. I can feel sympathy for Willie Horton for being in jail for the rest of his life.
> NEWT GINGRICH *in 1989, shortly after his efforts to bring about Jim Wright's downfall succeeded, with Wright's resignation as House Speaker*

The Democrats in the [Capitol] building get up every morning knowing that to survive they need to do only two things: They lie regularly and they cheat.

NEWT GINGRICH *in 1989*

[Mario Cuomo is] the most articulate spokesman of the pre-perestroika, Brezhnev wing of the Democratic Party.

NEWT GINGRICH *in 1990, on New York governor Cuomo*

George Mitchell is to the left of Yeltsin.

NEWT GINGRICH *in 1991, comparing the Democratic Senate majority leader to Russian president Boris Yeltsin*

I call this the Woody Allen plank. It's a weird situation, and it fits the Democratic Party platform perfectly. If a Democrat used the word "family" to raise children in Madison Square Garden, half their party would have rebelled, and the other half would not vote. Woody Allen had non-incest with his non-daughter because they were a non-family.

NEWT GINGRICH *in 1992, on the platform adopted by that year's Democratic National Convention*

If Thomas Edison had invented the electric light in the age of the welfare state, the Democrats would immediately introduce a bill to protect the candlemaking industry. The Democratic ticket would propose a tax on electricity—in fact, Al Gore does propose a tax on electricity. Ralph Nader would warn that electricity can kill; and at least one news report would begin, "The candlemaking industry was threatened today."

NEWT GINGRICH, *in his speech at the 1992 Republican National Convention*

Now, there are two salient facts about our next choice. . . . Fact No. 1 is for four years he's [President Bush] gone to a pharmacy controlled by Democrats, and the Democrats have given him no medicine or they've given him bad medicine. Fact No. 2, the alternative doctors in town, Dr. Feelgood and Dr. Smilegood, are nice young guys, [they] have a terrific guaranteed quick diet plan, 28-pound weight loss. The problem is, when you read the fine print, they get to the weight loss by amputating your leg. And the question is: Am I really eager enough to have a chance that I'll risk having my leg amputated?

NEWT GINGRICH *in 1992, dissing the Democratic ticket of* Clinton/Gore

[**I**n Al Gore's book *Earth in the Balance*], there's a paragraph where, having explained dysfunctionality for about six pages, he then explains the worst—he describes this terrible century as compared to Reagan's vision of the American century. He then compares the U.S. to a dysfunctional civilization . . . AstroTurf, plastic flowers, air conditioning, and frozen food from microwave ovens. I mean, it is just the sort of nutty left-wing goo-goo stuff.

NEWT GINGRICH *in 1992*

——————————— **Reality Check** ———————————

[The Democrats] promote a multicultural, nihilistic hedonism that is inherently destructive of a healthy society.

NEWT GINGRICH *in 1992 at the Republican National Convention*

On the one hand, there is a Republican Party that believes in opportunities and possibilities. On the other hand there is a Democratic Party that rejects the lessons of American history, despises the values of the American people, and denies the basic goodness of the American nation.

NEWT GINGRICH in 1994

My message [to the Democrats] is . . . "You want to avoid this kind of train wreck, you're going to call us in at the beginning . . . have conferences that are honest . . . and . . . do this thing with dignity. And, if you don't, every chance I get to wreck the train I'm going to wreck it. And when you get tired of looking stupid in public we'll talk.

NEWT GINGRICH in 1994, on battles over President Clinton's crime bill

The House Democrats are obsessed with me. It's almost funny how much they fear me.

NEWT GINGRICH in 1994

I clearly fascinate them.

NEWT GINGRICH in 1994, on Democrats' reaction to him

The price of trying to have historic change is to take historic risks. We had a good friend tell us the other week—somebody who knows the Clinton White House very intimately—"You should be mildly paranoid" because I really am Public Enemy Number One in the building. They just go nuts. But you can't be mildly paranoid and be effective.

NEWT GINGRICH in 1994

I thought Stephanopoulos would have just as soon shot all of us.

NEWT GINGRICH *in 1994, saying presidential adviser George Stephanopoulos and his White House colleagues tried to freeze Congressional Republicans out of negotiations during passage of the 1994 crime bill*

If I announced today I was buying vanilla ice cream for every child in America, David Bonior would jump up and say, "He wants them all to have heart attacks."

NEWT GINGRICH *in 1994, on Democratic House minority whip David Bonior, his chief tormentor in the controversy over Gingrich's multimillion-dollar book contract*

I am a genuine revolutionary; they are the genuine reactionaries. They will do anything to stop us, they will use any tool, there is no grotesquerie, no distortion, no dishonesty too great for them to come after us.

NEWT GINGRICH *in 1995, warning fellow Republicans of looming battle with Democrats opposed to his proposed "Contract With America" legislation*

I won't mention which Democrats I was thinking of when I looked over at some of them.

NEWT GINGRICH *in 1995, confessing he once wanted to be a zoo director, beaming after letting some exotic insects called Madagascar hissing cockroaches caper in his House Speaker's office*

On the GOP

The only hope we have to build an effective conservative majority is to use the Republican Party as our vehicle. I do not suggest that it is an ideal choice. The last two campaigns have proven to me personally that I run each time with a 700-pound elephant on my back as a handicap.

NEWT GINGRICH *at a 1977 fund-raiser in Atlanta*

In my lifetime—literally my lifetime, I was born in 1943—we have not had a competent national Republican leader. Never!

NEWT GINGRICH *in 1978, to College Republicans in Atlanta*

─────────── **Reality Check** ───────────

One of the great problems in the Republican Party is that we don't encourage you to be nasty. We encourage you to be neat, obedient, and loyal and faithful, and all those Boy Scout words, which would be great around the campfire, but are lousy in politics.

NEWT GINGRICH *in 1978, in a speech to*
College Republicans

I'm not very worried about it. It's a little bit like Republicans deciding to campaign as the most compassionate and caring advocates of the poor. Even if it were true, people's instinct is not to believe it.

NEWT GINGRICH *in 1995, on President Clinton's TV advertising campaign in support of his ban on the sales of certain assault weapons*

Media Man

TV news directors [are] *real* important. Incredibly important. That's the central nervous system. They're the ones who make the decision to put Gingrich on. If we can do "Face the Nation," that's *very* valuable.

NEWT GINGRICH *in 1985, reveling in his growing news-celebrity status*

I'm one of the leading speakers on Nicaragua. I am not a gadfly.

NEWT GINGRICH *in 1985, responding to the* Atlanta Journal's *suggestion that he lacked experience in foreign policy*

C-Span is more real than being there.

NEWT GINGRICH *in 1985, on the Congressional television channel*

In every election in American history, both parties have their cliches. The party that has the cliches that ring true wins. And if the cliches continue to ring true when the party governs, then that party and those cliches can change history.

NEWT GINGRICH *in 1988*

Practice whatever the big truth is so that you can say it in
40 seconds on camera.

> NEWT GINGRICH *in 1989, with advice to Republican*
> *members of Congress*

———————————— ♦ ————————————

I'm a controversial guy. . . . [I'm] reshaping the entire nation through
the news media.

> NEWT GINGRICH *in 1989*

If you're not in *The Washington Post* every day, you might as well not
exist.

> NEWT GINGRICH *in 1989*

Since I was nine, I've been oriented toward facilitating the media.

> NEWT GINGRICH *in 1991, on the newspaper article he wrote as a*
> *youth asking the mayor of his native Harrisburg, Pennsylvania, to*
> *establish a local zoo*

I've done very few things that were hip shots in my career. The style of
being aggressive enough and different enough when you guys cover me
is conscious.

> NEWT GINGRICH *in 1993*

Reality Check

I personally do not intend to stay in a politics that is
dominated by smearing and mud-slinging—a politics
which has all too often been characteristic of recent years
in this century.

NEWT GINGRICH *in a 1983 Congressional address*

♦

People are not in general stupid, but they are often ignorant. In their
ignorance they often tolerate ignorant news reporters who in turn
tolerate ignorant politicians. The result is an ignorant politician
making an ignorant speech to be covered by an ignorant reporter and
shown in a 40-second clip on television to an ignorant audience.

NEWT GINGRICH

You have to give the press confrontations. When you give them
confrontations, you get attention; when you get attention, you
can educate.

NEWT GINGRICH *in 1994*

Why should I announce that I do not want to be the nominee so that
none of you would pay attention to me? I am getting a better ride out
of your confusion than I ever got out of your coverage.

NEWT GINGRICH *in 1995, on his whirlwind book tour of New*
Hampshire, an important primary state, during which he was coy
about his presidential ambitions

I decided to be cynical. What I've learned is, if I keep the door open just this much, they'll all show up. And I could teach. And they'll actually cover it. They'll go, 'Ah-hah! This is a very sneaky way to run for President.'"

> NEWT GINGRICH *in 1995 on his New Hampshire media blitz*

What Others Say About Him

There is the Newt Gingrich who is the intellectual, appealing and fun to be with. And there's the Newt Gingrich who is the bloodthirsty partisan who'd just as soon cut your guts out as look at you.

> LEE HOWELL, *former Gingrich press secretary*

Newt wins all the marbles, then he puts the pillow over my head when I'm on life support. And he does it with a lie.

> LARRY LAROCCO, *defeated Idaho congressman, in 1994, complaining that after the Congressional elections, Newt Gingrich accused him of being charged with sexual harassment. The case in fact involved allegations of sex discrimination.*

I can still hold up the picture of me with Newt, like a cross before a vampire.

> SUSAN HILL, *operator of a chain of abortion clinics called the National Women's Health Organization, in 1995. In 1989, while in Washington to participate in an abortion rights demonstration, Hill and two of her consultants visited pro-life congressman Newt Gingrich and, without telling him why they were in Washington, succeeded in*

their request that he pose for a picture with them—a photo that Hill
said she now intends to display at her clinics in order to discourage
vandals and anti-abortion protesters.

Reality Check

[He's] the least substantive *major* legislator. There are
members of any legislative body who can be differentiated
from streetlights only because their noses don't light up.
Representative BARNEY FRANK (D–Mass.) *in 1995,*
when reminded that he had said that Newt Gingrich is the
least substantive legislator he had ever seen

◆

He might be in the other 10%.
JOYCELYN ELDERS, *former surgeon general, in 1995, on where Newt*
Gingrich might place in studies showing that 90% of Americans
masturbate. Elders was forced to resign her post in 1994 after
remarking that masturbation "perhaps should be taught."

Reality Check

Newt is a tad like Gandhi, a combination of visionary and
practical tactician not too often seen in politics. But
obviously, Gandhi dressed better.
TONY BLANKLEY, *spokesman for Newt Gingrich,*
in 1995

◆

Newtie is a talker.
> KATHLEEN GINGRICH, *the new House Speaker's mom, in 1995*

We had oral sex. He prefers that modus operandi because then he can say, "I never slept with her."
> ANNE MANNING, *a volunteer in Newt Gingrich's unsuccessful 1976 congressional campaign, in a 1995 interview with* Vanity Fair *magazine, alleging an adulterous 1977 assignation with the future House Speaker*

He can't do it without me. I told him if I'm not in agreement, fine, it's easy. I just go on the air the next day, and I undermine everything. . . . I don't want him to be president and I don't think he should be.
> MARIANNE GINGRICH *in 1995, on why she would sabotage any effort by her husband, Newt, to seek the presidency. "The presidency is not a single person," Marianne added. "It's not so much what he'd be doing. It's what I'd be doing."*

There's a similarity between Newt and Hitler. Hitler started out getting rid of the poor and those he said were a drag on society, and Newt is starting out the same way. I want to see how far Americans will let him and his young Republican cohorts take them up that ladder.
> *Representative* EARL HILLIARD *(D–Georgia) in 1995, on the cutback elements of the GOP's "Contract With America"*

He's one of the most original minds in American politics. But I think he would be the first to admit that he is just beginning to educate himself on foreign policy.

HENRY KISSINGER, *informal foreign policy adviser to Newt Gingrich, in 1995, after Gingrich's spate of off-the-cuff observations that, for instance, the only way to change Iran's cultural outlook was to have its government overthrown, that it won't be long before Iraq's Saddam Hussein and 20 computer hackers try to sabotage U.S. commerce by feeding in false American Express numbers, and that U.S. soldiers will be equipped in the not-too-distant future with satellite-linked telephones so that during lulls in battle they will be able to arrange a date or remind their home computer to water the plants. After his faux pas in calling for U.S. recognition of Taiwan over China's objections, which he reversed within days of the comment, Gingrich recalls that, "Henry [Kissinger] called me and said, 'This is not good.' I said, 'I wanted to have their attention.' He said, 'You have their attention.' "*

Author, Author!

Martel smiled as he thought about him. He hadn't been the cleverest flight leader in the fleet, but by God he knew how to lead a group straight into enemy flank like they were on rails. What was his name? . . . Lieutenant George Bush. Quite a guy, in his goofy way.

Passage from an unpublished novel cowritten by NEWT GINGRICH

I'm not going to be a masochist and say, "Please give me the lowest possible rate," so that *The New York Times* editorial board thinks I'm okay.

> NEWT GINGRICH *in 1994, on his decision to return most of the $4.5 million advance from his book deal but earn a higher royalty rate on sales*

Conservative books sell. I can't help it if liberal books don't sell.

> NEWT GINGRICH *in 1994, defending his lucrative book deal*

Book envy.

> NEWT GINGRICH's *term, in 1994, for the affliction suffered by critics of his multimillion-dollar book contract*

[Mine will be] way less boring than Al Gore's.

> NEWT GINGRICH *in 1995, shaking off criticism of his deal to publish his memoirs, insisting that his volume at least would have the virtue of being more interesting than Al Gore's eco-scare treatise* Earth in the Balance

Even though it had been only minutes since their last lovemaking, [he] was as ever overwhelmed by the sight of her, the shameless pleasure she took in her own body and its effect on him. Still, he mustn't let her see just how much she moved him. A relationship had to have some balance. He stretched in turn, reached over for his cigarettes and gold-plated Ronson on the Art Deco night stand with its Tiffany lamp. Since he wasn't sure what to say, he made a production of lighting up and enjoying that first, luxurious after-bout inhalation.

His continued silence earned him a small punishment.

"Darling . . . isn't it time for you to leave?"

Playfully, to drive home the potential loss, she bit his shoulder, then kissed it better.

"Aw, hell, I don't want to. . . . I wish I could just divorce Mrs. Little Goodie Two-Shoes!"

"I like this arrangement," she laughed softly. "Mistress to the chief of staff of the president of the United States. Nice title, don't you think? Such a book I could write." . . . Suddenly the pouting sex kitten gave way to Diana the Huntress. She rolled onto him and somehow was sitting athwart his chest, her knees pinning his shoulders. "Tell me, or I will make you do terrible things," she hissed.

> Excerpt from 1945, a novel coauthored by NEWT GINGRICH, as reported in The New York Times Magazine in December 1994. In response to criticism of 1945 from Bob Dole and others, Gingrich made some modifications. For instance, the following passage was omitted: "Suddenly the pouting sex kitten . . . make you do terrible things." It was replaced with " 'Tell me,' she hissed. Mayhew looked at his delicious interrogator."

Richer popped the magazine out of his Luger as he gazed tenderly down at the half-dozen girls he had just talked out of their hiding place and then killed. It had felt so wonderfully good, especially when the extremely pretty one started to cry as, after first forcing them to kneel, he systematically shot her five friends, one after another. [And] after she learned what was going to happen to her, she begged to be shot like the rest.

> Excerpt from 1945 that survived the prepublication criticism, describing the sadistic pleasures of an SS officer

The Futurist

Provisions for the government of space territories, including constitutional protections, the right to self-government and admission to statehood.

NEWT GINGRICH in an unsuccessful 1981 bill he sponsored, the National Space and Aeronautics Policy Act, Title 4 of which makes the above futuristic stipulations

A mirror system in space could provide the light equivalent of many full moons so that there would be no need for nighttime lighting of the highways. Ambient light covering entire areas could reduce the current danger of criminals lurking in darkness.

NEWT GINGRICH in 1984. As chairman of the Congressional Space Caucus, which was created at his initiative, Gingrich argued that space exploration could save the world from its most severe problems.

As people grow wealthier and the cost of space transportation comes down, spending a week's vacation on a space station or a honeymoon on the moon may become commonplace. People aboard space shuttles—the DC-3s of the future—will fly out to the Hiltons and Marriotts of the solar system, and mankind will have permanently broken free of the planet.

NEWT GINGRICH in 1985

Reality Check

Of course. How can one not be a Trekkie? I've spoken at the World Science Fiction Convention twice.

> NEWT GINGRICH *in 1994, when asked if he is a fan of the TV series "Star Trek." Asked if he believes in space aliens, Gingrich allowed, "It's mathematically plausible."*

♦

In a sense, virtuality at the mental level is something I think you'd find in most leadership over historical periods. But in addition, the thing . . . that I find fascinating is that we are not at a new place. It is just becoming harder and harder to avoid the place we are.

NEWT GINGRICH, *whose Internet address in 1995 is*
"georgia@hr.house.gov"

Master of Predictions

The United States is in greater danger from foreign powers than at any time since the British burned the capital in 1814. American foreign policy is increasingly confused and ineffective.

NEWT GINGRICH *in 1976*

If, in fact, we are to follow the Chamberlain liberal Democratic line of withdrawal from the planet, we would truly have tyranny everywhere and we in America could experience the joys of Soviet-style brutality and murdering of women and children.

NEWT GINGRICH *in a 1983 Congressional address*

We must expect the Soviet system to survive in its present brutish form for a very long time. There will be Soviet labor camps and Soviet torture chambers well into our great-grandchildren's lives; great centers of political and economic power have enormous staying power; Czarist Russia lasted through three and a half years of the most agonizing kind of war; the Nazi state did not collapse even when battlefield defeats reduced its control to only a tiny sliver of Germany.

NEWT GINGRICH *in 1984*

It is perfectly American to be wrong.

NEWT GINGRICH *in 1984*

----------------------- ◆ -----------------------

If I were betting, I would bet that by late next summer, George Bush will be a very formidable candidate, and I would bet a lot that he will be elected president.

NEWT GINGRICH *in 1991*

Very Well, I Contradict Myself

Does he mean this:

I am a moderate.

NEWT GINGRICH *to reporters in Atlanta on the night in 1978 when he won his first election to Congress*

Or this:

I am essentially a revolutionary.

NEWT GINGRICH *in 1992*

Does he mean this:

I'm a creature of the House.

> NEWT GINGRICH *in 1993, proud upholder of the traditions of the*
> *House of Representatives*

Or this:

The House is a corrupt institution.

> NEWT GINGRICH *in 1989*

Does he mean this:

When elected, Newt will keep his family together.

> *Congressional campaign ad for Newt Gingrich in 1978. Democratic*
> *opponent Virginia Shapard had said she planned to move to*
> *Washington if elected, leaving her family behind in Georgia.*

Or this:

She's not young enough or pretty enough to be the wife of a president.
And besides, she has cancer.

> *Attributed to* NEWT GINGRICH *as a comment he made on divorcing*
> *his first wife, said to have been made to former aide Kip Carter.*
> *Gingrich denies making the comment.*

Does he mean this:

The thing that shocks people . . . is that I mean what I say. I don't use hyperbole.

NEWT GINGRICH in 1989

Or this:

If the federal government had improved in efficiency as much as the computer has since 1950, we'd only need four federal employees and the federal budget would be $100,000.

NEWT GINGRICH, in his Renewing American Civilization
lecture series

Does he mean this:

This is really hard, making this happen—educating, reeducating, over and over, making a mistake, having to reanalyze. I'm trying to educate a nation in the skills of self-government.

NEWT GINGRICH in 1994

Or this:

Don't try to educate them [the voters]; that is not your job. You're in the politics business.

NEWT GINGRICH in 1978, to College Republicans in Atlanta

Does he mean this:

Our liberal national elite doesn't believe in religion.

NEWT GINGRICH in 1984

Or this:

I'm not a strong believer.

> NEWT GINGRICH *in 1984, on his instructions to a speechwriter to remove all references to God*

Or this:

I do have a vision of an America in which a belief in the Creator is once again at the center of defining being an American.

> NEWT GINGRICH *in 1995*

Does he mean this:

Perseverance is the hard work you do after you get tired of doing the hard work you already did. Perseverance is what you do when the seventh girl turned you down for dancing and you go to the eighth girl—or boy in the modern era.

> NEWT GINGRICH, *in his Renewing American Civilization lecture series*

Or this:

I'm the guy in the eighth grade who did not go across the floor and ask the girl to dance for two reasons. One is, she might say no and I'd be embarrassed; two, she might say yes, and I'd have to dance.

> NEWT GINGRICH *in 1985*

Does he mean this?

I just want to be blunt. I mean, this is a Democratic machine political scandal. Both in the House bank, which was a patronage operation, and in the House post office.

> NEWT GINGRICH *in 1992. Gingrich himself had overdrafts for 22 checks, one for $9,463 sent to the Internal Revenue Service.*

Does he mean this:

These people are sick. They are destructive of the values we believe in. They are so consumed by their own power, by a Mussolini-like ego, that their willingness to run over normal human beings and to destroy honest institutions is unending.

> NEWT GINGRICH *in 1989, on liberal Democrats*

And this:

Democrats are the enemy of normal Americans.

> NEWT GINGRICH *in 1994*

Or this:

The greatest leaders in fighting for an integrated America in the twentieth century were in the Democratic Party. The fact is, it was the liberal wing of the Democratic Party that ended segregation. The fact is that it was Franklin Delano Roosevelt who gave hope to a nation that was in despair and could have slid into dictatorship. And the fact is, every Republican has much to learn from studying what Democrats did right.

> NEWT GINGRICH *in 1995, in his inaugural speech as House Speaker*

Does he mean this:

I'm just tossing this out . . . but maybe we need a tax credit for the poorest Americans to buy a laptop.

> NEWT GINGRICH *in 1995, in testimony to the House Ways and Means Committee*

Or this:

[It was perhaps] a dumb idea.

> NEWT GINGRICH *in 1995, on his proposal to provide laptop computers to children*

Does he mean this:

[He's] the tax collector for the welfare state.

> NEWT GINGRICH *in 1985, on Senator Bob Dole*

And this:

Now we have to destroy Bob Dole.

> NEWT GINGRICH *after winning control of the House of Representatives in November 1994, saying his chief adversary now wasn't the president but his own GOP counterpart in the Senate*

Or this:

Bob Dole [is] unequivocally the hardest-working and, I think, an extraordinarily effective Republican leader.

> NEWT GINGRICH *in 1994*

Does he mean this:

You've got scattered throughout this administration counterculture people. . . . [I] had a senior law-enforcement official tell me that in his judgment, up to a quarter of the White House staff, when they first came in, had used drugs in the last four or five years.

NEWT GINGRICH *in 1994, on the Clinton White House, elaborating in a "Meet the Press" appearance on his charge that President Bill Clinton and his wife, Hillary Rodham Clinton, were "counterculture McGoverniks"*

Or this:

If I had to do it over again, I probably wouldn't have said it. I was still too much the assistant professor."

NEWT GINGRICH *in 1994, apologizing for calling the Clintons counterculturists*

And this:

I have to say as a Republican and as a conservative, I think the press has, overall, been very tough on the president and on Mrs. Clinton.

NEWT GINGRICH *in 1994*

Does he mean this?

I was trying to rattle their cage, to get their attention. I don't think we should recognize Taiwan.

NEWT GINGRICH *in 1995, days after a Face the Nation interviewer put him on the spot with a question for which he wasn't* prepared: *Should the U.S. recognize Taiwan over the long-standing objections of China?* Responding to the uproar from his assertion that the U.S. should recognize Taiwan, Gingrich quickly reversed himself, and added, *"I don't particularly care about having said the thing about Taiwan either way."*

·7·

Gramm-Standing

Gramm-standing.

> *A term for opposing a project for one's state on the grounds of exorbitant cost; then, after the measure has been approved over one's objections, calling a news conference to claim credit for securing the federal largesse on behalf of one's constituents—a practice perfected by Texas senator Phil Gramm*

I keep it in a quart jar on my desk.

> *Senator* PHIL GRAMM, *assuring a dinner audience that he does, in fact, have a heart, but tries not to let it unduly influence his policies*

Balancing the budget is like going to heaven. Everybody wants to do it, but nobody wants to make the trip.

> PHIL GRAMM, *who between 1991 and 1992 was one of only three lawmakers who did not sponsor a bill that cut spending*

Everybody's mother is on Medicare. Obviously she is grateful.

PHIL GRAMM, *a frequent critic of government-sponsored "Democrat, socialized" health care, in 1994, when reminded that his own mother enjoys Medicare coverage*

I've never said Government is all bad.

PHIL GRAMM, *who was born on a military post, whose education was partly funded by his father's GI insurance, and who went to graduate school on a National Defense Fellowship (he later voted to cut GI insurance and the NDF)*

I'm carrying so much pork I'm beginning to get trichinosis.

PHIL GRAMM, *acknowledging that his efforts to direct federal funds to his home state have been tireless*

People will be hunting Democrats with dogs by the end of the century.

PHIL GRAMM *in 1993, on what will happen if the Clinton administration's proposals become law*

Looking at [Clinton's] economic program . . . I feel like a mosquito in a nudist colony. The real question is where to strike first.

PHIL GRAMM *in 1993, on the many opportunities for attack presented by Bill Clinton's proposed deficit-reduction plan. In response, Senator Bob Kerrey said of Gramm, "[He's more like] a nudist in a mosquito colony, not knowing what to hide first."*

We have to blow up this train and the rails and trestle and kill everyone on board.

PHIL GRAMM *on the need to crush the Clinton administration's proposed health-care reforms*

I feel so sorry for your many problems, but you deserve them.

PHIL GRAMM, *in a letter to longtime political foe Representative Chet Edwards (D–Tex.)*

Most people don't have the luxury of living to be 80 years old, so it's hard for me to feel sorry for them.

PHIL GRAMM *in 1994, opposing expensive medical treatment for the old*

We're the only nation in the world where all our poor people are fat.

PHIL GRAMM *in 1994, opposing extravagant distribution of food stamps for the poor*

Sophia Loren is not a citizen.

PHIL GRAMM *in 1995, on whether he would choose a woman as his presidential running mate*

I was conservative before it was cool to be conservative.

      PHIL GRAMM, *announcing his presidential bid in February 1995.*
When it was cool to be a Democrat, in a Democrat-controlled
Senate, Gramm was one of those, too, switching in 1982 to the GOP,
which by that point had taken control of the Senate.

We are one victory away from getting our money back.
> PHIL GRAMM *in 1995, at his $4.5 million presidential fund-raising*
> *event in Texas*

─────────── **Reality Check** ───────────

I have the most reliable friend you can have in American politics and that is ready money.
> PHIL GRAMM *in 1995, forecasting his favorable*
> *prospects in the 1996 presidential race*

───────────── ◆ ─────────────

You haven't thought about a new husband, have you? I'm just kidding.
> PHIL GRAMM *to an elderly black widow in Corsicana, Texas, who*
> *told him that proposals to cut Social Security and Medicare would*
> *threaten the ability of older people like herself to retain their*
> *financial independence*

◆ 8 ◆

Guru Madness

All I know are two things—first, we have to beat Dewey, and second, Eisenhower beat Hitler. What else is there to know?

> ALEX ROSE, *activist in the New York Liberal Party, in 1948, when asked why he favored having the Democrats dump incumbent president Harry Truman as their presidential candidate in favor of Dwight Eisenhower, despite the general's having revealed his position on none of the major issues of the day*

—— Reality Check ——

I see that a speaker at the weekend said that this was a time when leaders should keep their ears to the ground. All I can say is that the British nation will find it very hard to look up to leaders who are detected in that somewhat ungainly posture.

WINSTON CHURCHILL

◆

Polls are for dogs.

Canadian prime minister JOHN DIEFENBAKER

One day the don't-knows will get in, and then where will we be?
British author SPIKE MILLIGAN *of* "Goon Show" *fame, on a preelection poll*

I'm not going to respond to that guy. In college, I understand they hooked him up to jumper cables.
LEE ATWATER *in 1980, responding to allegations by South Carolina attorney Tom Turnipseed that Atwater was using telephone pollsters to falsely inform voters that Turnipseed was an NAACP member on behalf of Atwater's client, Representative Floyd Spence (R–S.C.), who successfully overcame Turnipseed's bid to unseat him in a Congressional race. (Turnipseed had undergone electroshock therapy in his youth.) In 1991, Atwater, who had just stepped down as chairman of the Republican National Committee after undergoing treatment for a brain tumor, apologized to Turnipseed, saying, "My illness has taught me something about the nature of humanity, love, brotherhood, and relationships that I never understood and probably never would have."*

Governor?

Yeah?

It's nine o'clock.

Yeah?

Well, you're going to be inaugurated in two hours.

Does that mean I have to get up?
Exchange between MICHAEL DEAVER *and* RONALD REAGAN *on the morning of Reagan's first inauguration as president in 1981, as recalled by Deaver, a confidante of Reagan since his days as California governor*

So in the NBC debate, Gephardt takes out a .357 Magnum, and blows Bambi's head off.

> JOE TRIPPI, *adviser to Representative Richard Gephardt, candidate for the Democratic presidential nomination, in 1988, on the need to come down hard on his deceptively mild-mannered rival, Paul (Bambi) Simon, Democratic senator from Illinois*

Don't ever wear that shirt again! You looked like a f——g CLERK!

> *Political image adviser* ROGER AILES, *in 1987, to his client George Bush at the conclusion of a Bush speaking event in which the vice president peeled off his jacket to reveal a shirt with short sleeves*

What's Bob Dole going to do? Rent a trailer and invite all the New Hampshire Police Chiefs down to see him in his Airstream?

> LEE ATWATER, *campaign adviser to George Bush, in 1987, defending the Bush practice of inviting friends to the Bush family compound at Kennebunkport, Maine, while GOP presidential rival Bob Dole was attempting to project a common-man image*

———— Reality Check ————

The biggest differences between selling Brian Mulroney and selling soap are that soap doesn't talk and its competitors don't say it's a crock of s——.

> *Pollster* ALLAN GREGG *in 1989, on his work in helping get Canadian prime minister Brian Mulroney reelected in 1988*

That guy needs to go on Slim-Fast.

> ROSS PEROT *in 1992, describing Roger Ailes, after the heavyset*
> *Republican media consultant called him a "nut case." In reply, Ailes*
> *said, "I could drink some Slim-Fast, lose a few pounds. But when*
> *they lower his scrawny little rear into the ground, he's still going to*
> *be nuts."*

Gee, it's really a good thing we're not interested in him, because
he's dead.

> ED ROLLINS, *former Ross Perot campaign manager, in 1992,*
> *recalling his reaction when Perot advisers told him they had decided*
> *against the late William French Smith as a Perot running mate*

Sometimes it's hard to detach my James from the guy whose face I'd
like to rip off.

> MARY MATALIN, *political director of the Bush reelection campaign, in*
> *1992, on fiance and Clinton adviser James Carville, whom she*
> *nicknamed "Serpenthead"*

I wouldn't piss down his throat if his heart was on fire.

> JAMES CARVILLE *in 1992, on the regard in which he held an aide to*
> *would-be Democratic presidential nominee Jerry Brown*

------------- **Reality Check** -------------

It's hard for somebody to hit you when you've got your fist
in their face.

> JAMES CARVILLE, *on the usefulness of negative campaigning*

Well, dammit, I didn't get State. That's it. I quit. I got nothing left to do with these people.

> JAMES CARVILLE *in 1993, emerging from a session in which nominees*
> *for important cabinet posts in the Clinton administration were*
> *being selected*

--------------------- **Reality Check** ---------------------

Politics is show business for ugly people.

> PAUL BEGALA, *campaign adviser to Bill Clinton,*
> *in 1993*

------------------------------- ◆ -------------------------------

One thing I respect about Ed is that he doesn't leak. . . . He does more damage on the record than any leaker that I've ever seen.

> JIM LAKE, *Republican consultant, in 1993, on GOP strategist*
> *Ed Rollins's statement that the campaign team he managed for New*
> *Jersey gubernatorial winner Christine Todd Whitman had paid black*
> *ministers and others to discourage black voter turnout*

There are three and a half billion Asians who don't know Ed Rollins.

> ED ROLLINS *in 1994, explaining why he planned to focus on*
> *international consulting in the aftermath of gaffes at home in the*
> *United States*

It's like how many blacks you played on the basketball team in Louisiana 20 years ago. The rule was: three at home, four on the road, and five when you're behind.

JAMES CARVILLE, *campaign adviser to Bill Clinton, in 1993, on why the White House was recruiting so many former campaign staffers to avoid repetition of blunders that had plagued the new administration*

You drag $100 bills through trailer parks, there's no tellin' what you'll find. I know these people. I went to school with 'em. I necked with 'em in back seats, spent nights with 'em.

JAMES CARVILLE *in 1994, on women who claimed they slept with Bill Clinton*

To me, the best candidate of all would be an astronaut. He can say, "I was floating in outer space the whole time."

GOP *pollster* FRANK LUNTZ *in 1994, on the advantages of being a political outsider*

The only thing I ever pick is my nose.

JAMES CARVILLE *in 1994, when asked on "Meet the Press" for his predictions on the outcome of the 1994 Congressional elections*

Whitewater is not about cover-ups, it's about screw-ups.

DAVID GERGEN, *White House image counsellor, in 1994, on the difference between Watergate and Whitewater*

Returning to Washington today really brought back memories. As our plane headed to the airport, I looked down on the White House and it was just like the good old days—the South Lawn, the Rose Garden. And David Gergen.

> RONALD REAGAN *in 1994, at a GOP fund-raiser in honor of his 83rd birthday. Former Reagan adviser Gergen had joined the Clinton White House in an image-management capacity similar to his work for Reagan.*

Incompetence is always the excuse.

> MARY MATALIN, *GOP strategist, in 1994, after Democratic consultant Robert Squier blamed the Clinton administration's poor handling of the Whitewater affair on the fact that Democrats "have been out of the White House so long, we don't know quite how to act sometimes"*

─────────── **Reality Check** ───────────

Washington is Salem. If we're not lynching somebody 24 hours a day in this wretched town, we're not happy.

> TOM KOROLOGOS, *Washington lobbyist and Nixon White House veteran, in 1994*

───────────── ♦ ─────────────

"**P**owell! Vy didn't you tell us! Vy didn't you warn us? All kinds of politicians. They give speeches, and they shout and scream and they are reactionary and liars and thieves and crooks and criminals." And I say, "Welcome to democracy, babe! It's just like Washington. That's what it's all about. You're going to learn to live with it, and you're going to love it."

General COLIN POWELL, *who served in three administrations, in 1995, recalling conversations with former Russian foes who now seek his advice on democracy*

We're stringing up the electric chair here, but we didn't make him guilty; he made himself guilty.

STEVE JOST, *Democratic fund-raiser and a leader of a "get-Newt" movement, in 1995, on efforts to dig up and disseminate potentially embarrassing material on the new House Speaker, Newt Gingrich, by means of "Newtgram" mailings and Internet messages, including details of ethics investigations, donor lists, and even Gingrich's cosponsorship of "commemorative bills" such as National Quilting Day and National Convenience Store Appreciation Week*

If elected mayor of L.A., he could show those Hymie boys, Berman and Waxman, who were always trying to make Willie feel inferior for not being Jewish.

ED ROLLINS *in 1995, suggesting at a roast for California assembly speaker Willie Brown, who was contemplating a San Francisco mayoralty bid, that Brown would do better to run in Los Angeles, where he could one-up local Democratic congressmen Howard L. Berman and Henry A. Waxman. In the aftermath of criticism over the comment, Rollins resigned his post as an unpaid adviser to the Bob Dole presidential campaign.*

[**C**linton] is fundamentally mispositioned for 1996.

        Democratic pollster STAN GREENBERG *in 1995, in a memo urging President Bill Clinton to target working-class voters*

·9·

Foreign Affairs

I would be quite willing, personally, to leave that whole [Hudson's Bay Co.] country a wilderness for the next half century, but I fear if Englishmen do not go there, Yankees will.

JOHN A. MACDONALD, *first prime minister of Canada*

A great man? Why, he's selfish, he's arrogant, he thinks he's the center of the universe—yes, you're *right*. He *is* a great man!

WINSTON CHURCHILL *on Charles de Gaulle*

Belgium is a country invented by the British to annoy the French.

CHARLES DE GAULLE

No matter what happens, the U.S. Navy is not going to be caught napping.

FRANK KNOX, *secretary of the Navy, on December 4, 1941, three days before the Japanese raid on the U.S. naval base at Pearl Harbor*

He gave me a lot of hooey about how great my country is and how he loved Roosevelt and how he intended to love me, etc. Well . . . I am sure we can get along if he doesn't try to give me too much soft soap.

> President HARRY TRUMAN's *reaction after his first meeting with Winston Churchill*

I like Stalin. He is straightforward.

> PRESIDENT TRUMAN's *assessment of the Soviet dictator Joseph Stalin after their first meeting. Truman was amused to discover that Stalin, the self-described "Man of Steel," stood about 5'5"—"a little bit of a squirt," Truman thought.*

I haven't read Karl Marx, I got stuck on that footnote on page 2.

> *British prime minister and Labour Party leader* HAROLD WILSON, *who preferred whodunits to nonfiction*

Don't spread the story around. If you tell everybody that you like me better than [Richard] Nixon, I'll be ruined at home.

> President JOHN KENNEDY *in 1961, on receiving a warm greeting from Soviet leader Nikita Khrushchev during a Vienna summit*

No, Mr. Chancellor, I was born in a manger.

> President LYNDON JOHNSON, *to Germany's Ludwig Erhard, who had said, "I understand you were born in a log cabin."*

My rule in international affairs is, "Do unto others as they would do unto you."
President RICHARD NIXON *to Israeli prime minister Golda Meir.*
Henry Kissinger chimed in, "Plus 10%."

I'm surprised that a government organization could do it that quickly.
President JIMMY CARTER *in 1979, during a visit to Egypt, on being told that the Great Pyramid at Giza took 20 years to build*

We must have adequate professional forces to impose our will on the Third World. Let me repeat that, because it is a very unfashionable thing to say. . . . There are those moments in life when we are going to disagree with other people, and it is my belief that when we fundamentally disagree with someone we should win.
NEWT GINGRICH *in a 1980 Congressional address*

———————— **Reality Check** ————————

We have seen others swallowed by crocodiles, and we have learned from their mistakes.
King SOBHUZA II *of Swaziland, who held the throne for 60 years, before dying in 1982 at age 83*

———————— ♦ ————————

And I was with him, and I sensed, uh . . . Stop! . . . And we stopped. And he got out of the car. So, he controls the agenda. And I saw that, yeah.

> GEORGE BUSH *in 1988, responding to a reporter who asked the vice president to elaborate on his observation during a recent Moscow visit that Mikhail Gorbachev appeared to assert complete control over the Soviet government*

I am ashamed even to pronounce this word, "Condomat."

> *Rabbi* YOSEF BA-GAD, *Israeli legislator, in 1992, after a condom dispenser was installed in a parliamentary committee room as part of World AIDS Day*

There is no reason for that. I don't think they gave me a lobotomy, because it's not at that end that this happened.

> *French president* FRANÇOIS MITTERRAND *in 1992, on whether he might be forced to resign after surgery for prostate cancer*

My dog Millie knows more about foreign affairs than these two bozos.

> GEORGE BUSH *in 1992, on the Clinton-Gore ticket*

I thought this guy was kind of dead.

> GEORGE BUSH *in 1992, meeting with Israeli prime minister Yitzhak Rabin in Maine, on a protester's sign honoring assassinated right-wing Jewish leader Meir Kahane*

They'll turn it into hors d'oeuvres for Deng Xiaoping, who, I'm told, eats four puppies a day.

> GARETH EVANS, *Australian foreign minister, at a 1992 reception in Hong Kong, after hearing that Hong Kong governor Chris Patten's dog had been reported missing*

It's someone Kohl from Germany.

> *An aide at Bill Clinton's Little Rock campaign headquarters in 1992, when German chancellor Helmut Kohl telephoned to congratulate the new president-elect*

Not enough salt in the hamburger.

> *Russian president* BORIS YELTSIN *in 1993, appraising the Big Mac he sampled at a new McDonald's outlet in Moscow*

It's just like Pespi-Cola!

> EDUARD SHEVARDNADZE, *Georgian leader and former Soviet foreign minister, in 1993, after tasting Coca-Cola at the opening of a new Coke bottling plant in Tbilisi*

We will create new Hiroshimas and Nagasakis. I will not hesitate to deploy nuclear weapons. You know what Chernobyl meant for our country. You will get your own Chernobyl in Germany.

> VLADIMIR ZHIRINOVSKY, *Russian nationalist, in 1993, complaining about alleged German interference in Russian affairs, a few days after his party made major gains in parliamentary elections*

Everybody likes to go to Geneva. You'd find these potentates from down in Africa, you know—rather than eating each other, they'd just come up and get a good square meal in Geneva.

Senator ERNEST HOLLINGS (D–S.C.) *in 1993, on the attraction of international trade conferences—a remark that drew fire from the NAACP and other groups*

When I met John Major the other night, he slapped me on the back and said, "You know, you don't look anything like your passport photos."

President BILL CLINTON *in 1993, in a speech for TV and radio reporters. During the presidential race, the Bush administration had sought British government assistance in locating passport photographs of Clinton to determine his role, while a student in England, in protests against the war in Vietnam.*

I've never met Kim Campbell and Jean. . . . I just don't know your Prime Minister.

Self-professed foreign policy expert DAN QUAYLE *in 1994, promoting his memoirs in Toronto, seven months after Jean Chrétien had replaced Campbell as prime minister*

We've got 300 Minutemen III's in North Dakota that we're ready to retarget and maybe that will get their attention.

Senator KENT CONRAD (D–N.Dak.) *in 1994, suggesting an abrupt means of getting Canada to stop "excessive" exports of durum wheat to the United States*

My ambition in life isn't to go fishing with the president of the
United States.

> *Liberal Party of Canada leader* JEAN CHRÉTIEN *campaigning in
> 1993, disparaging former prime minister Brian Mulroney's close ties
> with Presidents Reagan and Bush.*

When Washington is awake, I am asleep. And even better, when I am awake, Washington is sleeping.

> WALTER MONDALE *in 1994, on the benefits of his new posting as*
> *U.S. ambassador to Japan*

Some president of the United States he is! Let him play his saxophone back home instead of coming here to meet with nobodies!

> *Russian political leader* VLADIMIR ZHIRINOVSKY *in 1994, after*
> *President Clinton said he would not meet with him during his trip*
> *to Moscow*

Look at how machismo works in Latin America. There are many countries where it is a good idea for the candidate in order to be elected to have a lot of girlfriends, where being a womanizer is a virtue.

> FIDEL CASTRO *in 1994, saying that inquiries into Bill Clinton's*
> *personal life are a "violation of his human rights"*

The United Nations is a totally incompetent instrument anyplace that matters. When you get a serious problem with serious violence, the United Nations is literally incompetent, and it kills people by its behavior.

> NEWT GINGRICH *in 1994*

Maybe their problem with the U.N. is that there are just too many foreigners there, but that really can't be helped.

> MADELEINE ALBRIGHT, *U.S. ambassador to the United Nations, in*
> *1995, on GOP attempts to cut U.S. funding of the United Nations*

Senator Helms: Now, Mrs. Harriman, I know that you are involved in the Monnet Society. [Jean] Monnet, of course, one of the spiritual founders of the European community?

Ms. Harriman: Senator, I do not think I am involved in the Monnet Society. I have never heard of it, frankly.

Senator Helms: I believe the information submitted says that. Is that not correct?

Ms. Harriman: Oh, it is *Claude Monet*, senator. It is the painter, the artist. His home is in France, it is called Giverny, where Claude Monet lived and painted. And I have given a contribution to . . . help restore his home.

> *From hearings of the Senate Foreign Relations Committee, of which Senator Jesse Helms is a member, on the nomination of Patricia Harriman as U.S. ambassador to France*

The Foreign Relations Committee has had the honor of welcoming the distinguished prime minister of India.

> *Senator* JESSE HELMS *in 1995, introducing Pakistani prime minister Benazir Bhutto on the floor of the Senate*

When I was in Washington recently to see Newt Gingrich, I was very pleased to have some of the New Republicans distancing themselves from me at the table. Pat Buchanan took his meal in an anteroom several blocks away. Being shunned because you're a moderate is a whole new life experience. And I therefore plan to visit some other extremists, just to further demonstrate my moderation by comparison.

> PRESTON MANNING, *leader of the Reform Party of Canada, in remarks to the 1995 Ottawa Press Gallery dinner*

I'm afraid I may have insulted some of our American friends [during a recent trip to Washington]. I told them that we Canadians don't believe in their Declaration of Independence, because we have our own Declaration of Dependence. Our Declaration reads: "We hold these truths to be self-evident, that all Canadians are created unequal. And are afflicted by their Creator with certain inalienable inequalities, for the removal of which God created—[Human Resources Minister] Lloyd Axworthy."

> PRESTON MANNING, *leader of the Reform Party of Canada, in*
> *remarks to the 1995 Ottawa Press Gallery dinner*

February 24, 1995

After receiving complaints from our citizens, we conducted an investigation and discovered that the owner of the company that distributes Dole bananas is Robert Dole, the United States senator who is waging an intensive campaign against Turkey.

The mayor of Izmir, Dr. Burhanettin Ozfatura, said it would not be in Turkey's national interest to purchase goods from a company owned by someone who is trying to blacken Turkey's name.

Officials of Tanasas, Izmir's municipally owned supermarket, said that Dole bananas will be removed from its seventeen stores and replaced with Chiquita and Bonita bananas.

February 26, 1995

The mayor said that he was misinformed about the ownership of the Dole company, and that the sale of Dole bananas would resume immediately. The mayor stated that the Ban had been useful, though, because it showed Americans that the Turkish public is very sensitive to foes of Turkey.

Statements issued by the office of Burhanettin Ozfatura, mayor of Izmir, a city in Western Turkey, in 1995, in reaction to Senator Bob Dole's effort to cut off additional aid to Turkey because of its blockade of humanitarian aid to Armenia

Except for his tendency to get angry, arrogant and sulky, he is the most qualified.

NOBORU TAKESHITA, former Japanese prime minister, in 1995, on trade minister Ryutaro Hashimoto's prospects for getting the prime minister's job

It would be the equivalent of having the prime minister of England invite the Oklahoma City bombers to 10 Downing Street, to congratulate them on a job well done.

Former British prime minister MARGARET THATCHER in 1995, on President Clinton's warm welcome of Sinn Fein leader Gerry Adams to the United States

Thank God I am a dreamer, and in spite of all the persecution, the litigation and the harassment they have done to me, I have not become a cynic.

IMELDA MARCOS, shoe collector and former first lady of the Philippines, in 1995, after standing for election even though she had been officially disqualified from holding office

·10·

That Whiff of Scandal

I think it's quite possible it was a truthful statement.
> BRENT SCOWCROFT, *national security adviser, in 1992, on George Bush's claim that he didn't actively oppose the Iran-contra arms-for-hostages deal because he didn't know all the facts*

Someone has restructured his memory.
> Clinton campaign adviser BETSEY WRIGHT *in 1992, on retired Arkansas ROTC Colonel Eugene Holmes. On Bill Clinton's efforts to join the ROTC program in 1969 to avoid the draft, Holmes had said, "I believe he purposely deceived me."*

The subject of impeachment was never openly discussed in the White House. It was a no-no word. You never used the word "impeachment" except to yourself.
> DONALD REGAN, *Reagan White House chief of staff, in 1993, on the climate in the official residence during the Iran-contra investigation*

So far, no one's offered movie rights on this.

> DAVID AXELROD, *Democratic consultant, in 1993, on the break-in at
> an office set up by the Democratic National Committee in a Chicago
> hotel where the Republican National Committee was meeting*

———————— **Reality Check** ————————

I am not sure but I have sometimes unnecessarily deprived
myself and others of innocent enjoyments.

> *President* RUTHERFORD B. HAYES, *on having adopted a
> puritanical aversion to simple pleasures in an age of
> widespread corruption among officeholders*

————————————— ◆ —————————————

I'm a politician, and as a politician I have the prerogative to lie
whenever I want.

> CHARLES PEACOCK, *an ex-director of Madison Guaranty, the
> Arkansas savings and loan at the center of the Whitewater
> investigation, in 1994, explaining why he lied about writing a check to
> help erase a Clinton gubernatorial debt*

They're doing a tin cup for Bill and Hillary, and any way you cut it, it's
unprecedented and it's not pretty.

> CHARLES LEWIS, *director of the Center for Public Integrity, in 1994,
> on the newly created legal defense fund for the Clintons with which the
> First Couple pays counsel to represent them in probes of their
> Whitewater real-estate investment and allegations of sexual
> harassment by Clinton filed by Paula Jones*

Had these ground rules applied in the O.J. Simpson trial, you couldn't ask him about the knife, you couldn't ask him about the glove, you couldn't ask him about the blood. All you could do is say, "How was your flight from Chicago?"

> GOP Representative TONY ROTH in 1994, insisting that Bill Clinton
> was unfairly protected by the limited scope of the Whitewater hearings
> in Congress

After all, the Republicans didn't bring about a suicide of a top presidential adviser.

> Representative JIM LEACH (R–Iowa) in 1994, insisting that his
> demand for a Whitewater probe and access to files on the deal
> removed from the office of the late White House counsellor Vince
> Foster were not politically motivated

You have to remember the position that all Republicans have been in for 12 years, where we were investigated, sometimes frivolously. If we get a chance to point a finger, why, it requires a saintliness that is superhuman, supernatural, to act with restraint.

> Representative HENRY HYDE (R–Ill.) in 1994, on the GOP's
> aggressive pursuit of Whitewater allegations

We have no statements to issue, we have no schedule, we have no bananas.

> JIM JAFFE, aide to Representative Dan Rostenkowski, in a message on
> the embattled congressman's telephone answering machine the day in
> 1994 that "Rosty" was indicted on corruption charges

You know, in Chicago we have a very unusual association with people that work for us.

> *Representative* DAN ROSTENKOWSKI *(D–Ill.) in 1994, defending himself against charges that he kept phantom employees on the payroll*

A good employee never questions anyone anyway.

> ANTHONY RAMIREZ *in 1994, on how he managed to be employed for nine years as a phantom worker in the office of Congressman Dan Rostenkowski*

———— Reality Check ————

That city could corrupt Saint Francis.

> MICHAEL FLANAGAN *in 1994, after winning Dan Rostenkowski's seat in the House, vowing to avoid the ethics problems that felled Rostenkowski, in part by serving no more than 10 years in Washington*

———————— ♦ ————————

I have lied in good faith.

> *French politician* BERNARD TAPIE *in 1995, after his sworn alibi crumbled in court. Tapie was accused of fixing a 1993 match involving the Marseilles soccer club he owned.*

Speaking of Sex . . .

My greatest enemy [will conclude] that there is nothing worse in the affair than an irregular and indelicate amour. For this, I bow to the just censure which it merits. I have paid pretty severely for the folly and can never recollect it without disgust and self-condemnation. It might seem affectation to say more.

> ALEXANDER HAMILTON, *first U.S. treasury secretary, in a 1797 letter aimed at clearing his name as a public figure by revealing an aspect of his private life. In response to a charge of paying off one Maria Reynolds as part of a scheme to speculate in government certificates, Hamilton admitted that he had conducted an affair with Reynolds, who was then married, and had paid $1,100 in hush money to her husband, a small-time criminal, but that he had in no way abused his trust as custodian of public funds. Hamilton was indeed innocent of financial conversion, and was widely admired for making a clear declaration of those personal misjudgments of which he was guilty.*

---———— **Reality Check** ————---

Three things ruin a man, power, money and women.
> HARRY TRUMAN, *a favorite saying*

———————— ♦ ————————

If I don't have a woman every three days or so I get a terrible headache.

> President JOHN KENNEDY, *in an aside to British prime minister Harold Macmillan*

I feel I'm the person responsible for putting Bill Clinton in the White House.

> GENNIFER FLOWERS *in 1993, asserting that her claim of an affair with*
> *Clinton gave him the crucial publicity lift that carried him into the*
> *White House*

I just didn't get it. I do now.

> *Senator* BOB PACKWOOD *in 1992, apologizing for his "offensive"*
> *behavior toward women accusing him of sexual harassment*

They don't call me Tyrannosaurus Sex for nothing!

> Senator EDWARD KENNEDY (D–Mass.), *spoken while wearing a*
> *Barney the Dinosaur costume at his 1993 office Christmas party*

If I asked her out, was I breaking the law? Would I end up on the front page?

> *Freshman representative* ERIC FINGERHUT, *33, in 1993, fretting*
> *about the perils of dating a former campaign worker after he was*
> *elected to the House*

I guess Bob Packwood was busy.

> *Senator* JOHN KERRY *(D–Mass.) in 1994, on the GOP's choice of*
> *Senator Alfonse D'Amato as its designated spokesperson on ethics.*
> *Packwood at the time faced a Senate inquiry into charges of sexual*
> *harassment, and D'Amato had only recently been cleared of charges*
> *that with his permission his brother had used the senator's office to*
> *conduct private business.*

Reality Check

Senator Porgie denies the allegations and claims all the women who have come forward to accuse him are making the whole thing up.

> *Message inside a greeting card tailored for working*
> *women, on sale in Washington, D.C., in 1995. The*
> *cover line reads: "Senator Porgie Pudding and Pie, kissed*
> *the girls and made them cry."*

It's getting ridiculous. It seems there's a policy of one bonk and you're out.

> *Anonymous British Tory cabinet minister in 1995, reacting to the news that Bank of England deputy governor Rupert Pennant-Rae had resigned after tabloid newspapers revealed his affair with an Irish-American journalist*

And Now a Word from My Sponsors . . .

Dear Mr. Galbraith:

It gives me great pleasure to inform you that at the last membership meeting of the Republican Senatorial Inner Circle, your name was placed in nomination by Senator John Chafee, and you were accepted for membership. . . .

Dear Mr. Vice President:

It was very nice, indeed, of Senator John Chafee to nominate me for membership in the "Republican Senatorial Inner Circle." I make haste to accept. . . .

You mention that there will be "closed door" briefings of the members of the Republican Inner Circle. . . . I wonder if some of those so selected may be paying money for this privilege, even though you have no intention of offering it. Doesn't this put you in a no-win situation? Either you are offering information for money-making purposes that is not available to the public at large or you are guilty of a certain fraud in giving the impression that there will be such advantage. I do hasten to assure you again that this does not trouble me in a personal way. I am not in business and will, of course, avoid making a contribution. . . .

Exchange of letters in 1989 between Vice President DAN QUAYLE *and Harvard economist and longtime Democrat* JOHN KENNETH GALBRAITH, *who served in the administrations of Franklin Roosevelt and John Kennedy. The 5,000 or so members of the Inner Circle, which was dedicated to bringing about a GOP majority in the Senate, were expected to contribute at least $1,000 per year in campaign assistance to GOP candidates.*

Dear Lt. Col. North:

I have read your pathetic letter in which you refer to Representative Ron Dellums as an "incredible security risk" and a "very dangerous appointment" to the U.S. House Select Committee on Intelligence. Frankly, Colonel, you are full of s——. . . .

For you to stoop to making such inflammatory, groundless attacks for the purposes of squeezing direct-mail dollars from a vulnerable mailing list is sick and pathetic. You ought to be ashamed.

Sincerely,

Pete Stark, U.S. Congressman

Response by Representative PETE STARK *(D–Calif.) in 1991 to Oliver North, on receiving a direct-mail solicitation in which North asked supporters to sign a petition against the appointment of Representative Ron Dellums (D–Calif.) and to make a donation to North's political organization, Freedom Alliance*

Elizabeth and I are especially excited about the news of your nomination because we will have the chance to be with you.

> *1991 letter signed by* BOB *and* ELIZABETH DOLE, *to rap star Eazy-E of gangsta rap group N.W.A. (Niggers With Attitude), informing him of his nomination to the Republican Senatorial Inner Circle. Eazy-E is a self-confessed "woman beater" and drug dealer.*

If my own mother had been alive, even she would not have voted for me.

> *Oklahoma representative* MICKEY EDWARDS *in 1992. Edwards, who lost in his own party's primary race, had bounced 386 checks at the House bank.*

Stop the power of the few.

> *Democratic presidential candidate* JERRY BROWN *in 1992, fretting about the influence of special-interest groups in government while being honored at a champagne breakfast paid for by Atlantic Richfield Co. and Southern California Edison*

--------------------- **Reality Check** ---------------------

This is the first time I ever got to see you without paying for it.

> WILL ROGERS, *on meeting President Warren Harding at the White House, in reference to the favor-seekers rampant at the time*

It is a very wonderful company; it does very interesting things.
>   NEWT GINGRICH *in one of his* Renewing American Civilization *videocassette lectures, on computer maker Hewlett-Packard Co., which donated $5,800 worth of equipment to Gingrich's political organizations*

Just like that, money started to pour in. I began feeling better, and my standing in the polls began to climb.
>   *Senator* BEN NIGHTHORSE CAMPBELL (D–Colo.) *in 1993, after members of his Northern Cheyenne tribe persuaded him to carry the tuft of an eagle feather and apply red paint to parts of his body to reverse a drop in poll ratings during the last stages of his 1992 election campaign*

This is all it costs to become mayor of New York City. Of course, there was that nine million and the five million before that. . . .
>   RUDOLPH GIULIANI *in 1994, paying the traditional 15-cent clerk's fee to take his oath of office as mayor of New York, on the cost of his two mayoral campaigns*

─────────── **Reality Check** ───────────

My first qualification for mayor of the City of New York is my monumental ingratitude to each and all of you.
>   FIORELLO LAGUARDIA, *shouted to his supporters from a table he leapt onto at his campaign headquarters on the night of his first election victory in 1933*

───────────── ♦ ─────────────

Writing a thank-you note to campaign contributors in today's climate forces me to emulate Rube Goldberg without pictures. . . . My job is to convey appreciation while affirming that this appreciation will remain wholly intangible and will never take any concrete form whatsoever. It is my task to assure you of my eternal gratitude for your contribution, while simultaneously making sure that everyone understands that I will be eternally unmindful of the fact that you have contributed when any public policy issue comes before me.

Representative BARNEY FRANK *(D–Mass.) in a 1994 form letter sent to contributors to his reelection campaign*

In the bible of campaign politics it says, "In the beginning was the word, the word was money." But the idea that there is some gargantuan amount of money that one must raise in order to be a competitive candidate for President remains to be proven.

HALEY BARBOUR, *chairman of the Republican National Committee, in 1995, commenting on early reports that GOP presidential candidates will be permitted by law to spend about $44 million each on the primary races and that an aggressive effort by presidential hopefuls to raise these funds from special interests at the same time they are attacking the curse of special-interest influence over Congress is polluting the democratic process*

·11·

Better Left Unsaid

There's nothing wrong with this country that we couldn't cure by turning it over to the police for a couple of weeks.

Georgia governor GEORGE WALLACE *in 1967*

——— Reality Check ———

It is dangerous for a national candidate to say things people might remember.

Senator EUGENE MCCARTHY

♦

This may be a false spring for liberals. Oklahoma City doesn't mean Americans are suddenly going to want big government.

NEWT GINGRICH *in 1995, attempting to counter the suggestion that the bombing of a federal building in Oklahoma City and the resulting deaths of scores of civil servants had produced a widespread appreciation of bureaucrats*

Judge Ito loves the limelight. He is making a disgrace of the judicial system. Little Judge Ito. For God's sake, get [the jurors] there for 12 hours; get this thing over. I mean, this is a disgrace. Judge Ito with the wet nose. And then he's going to have a hung jury. Judge Ito will keep us from getting television for the next year.

> Senator ALFONSE D'AMATO in 1995, on Don Imus's New York
> radio talk show, accepting Imus's invitation to complain—in an
> exaggerated Asian accent—that the televised trial of O.J. Simpson,
> presided over by Judge Lance Ito, would force D'Amato to reschedule
> his committee's hearings into the Whitewater affair if D'Amato had
> any hope of attracting an audience

It's my personal belief that if they're not rehabilitated after 15 years, kill 'em.

> State senator TIM JENNINGS (D–N.Mex.) in 1995, on what should
> be done with incorrigible prison inmates and criminals

———————— Reality Check ————————

America is the only nation in history which miraculously has gone directly from barbarism to degeneration without the usual interval of civilization.

> French political leader GEORGE CLEMENCEAU

————————— ♦ —————————

We in America are nearer to the final triumph over poverty than ever before in the history of the land. . . . We shall soon with the help of God be in sight of the day when poverty shall be banished from this nation.

> HERBERT HOOVER in 1928

The crisis will be over in 60 days.

> Statement issued in March 1930 by President HERBERT HOOVER and
> his cabinet, referring to the Great Depression. Other pronouncements
> followed: "Normal conditions should be restored in two or three
> months" (May 1930); "I am convinced we have now passed the
> worst" (May 1930); "The worst is over without a doubt" (June
> 1930); and "We have hit bottom and are on the upswing"
> (September 1930).

Reality Check

There's—a—mighty fine fishworm.

> Vice President CALVIN COOLIDGE, on being invited to
> say a few words after presiding at the spade-turning for a
> new public building

Career-Eliminating Comments

That's the first lunatic I've had for an engineer. He probably ought to
be shot at sunrise.

> THOMAS DEWEY campaigning for president in 1948, after his
> campaign train suddenly lurched a few feet backward at a whistlestop,
> causing a brief panic in the crowd. Dewey's icy comment was widely
> reported, and his lead over Truman in Gallop polling began to
> drop sharply.

[W]atergate should not be an issue] any more than the war in Vietnam would be . . . or World War II, or World War I, or the Korean War—*all Democrat wars* . . . all in this century. . . . I figured up, the other day: If we added up the killed and wounded in Democrat wars, in this century, it would be about 1.6 million Americans . . . enough to fill the city of Detroit!

> *Senator BOB DOLE, vice-presidential running mate to Gerald Ford, in 1976, debating his Democratic counterpart Walter Mondale. Dole later insisted that he merely didn't feel all Republicans should be tarred with Watergate any more than Democrats should be blamed for wars that happened to occur when Democrats controlled the White House.*

[A]s of now, I am in control now.

> *Secretary of State ALEXANDER HAIG in 1981, a few hours after the attempted assassination of President Ronald Reagan. The line of succession in fact runs through a few other people, including the vice president and the Speaker of the House, before reaching the secretary of state. On hearing of the comment, Nancy Reagan began her ultimately successful campaign to have Haig fired from the Reagan administration.*

[W]hy am I the only Biden in a thousand generations. . . .

> *Senator JOE BIDEN in a 1987 speech, while campaigning for the Democratic presidential nomination, repeating almost word for word a speech by British Labor Party leader Neil Kinnock that contained the rousing line "Why am I the only Kinnock in a thousand generations" to attend college? Coupled with accusations that he was plagiarizing speeches by Bobby Kennedy and rumors that he had cheated on law school exams, the speech triggered Biden's decision to drop out of the race.*

You people . . . *your* people . . .
> Ross Perot *in 1992, in a speech on racial harmony to a convention of the NAACP. After withdrawing from the presidential race on July 16, Perot was labeled by one observer, "The Yellow Ross of Texas."*

Reality Check

If you don't say anything, you won't be called on to repeat it.
> Calvin Coolidge

---◆---

You can't have a debate on such a key issue as the modernization of social programs in 47 days.
> Canadian Tory prime minister Kim Campbell *in 1993, campaigning for reelection; the subsequent resounding defeat of Campbell derived in part from this comment's suggestion that the voters lacked sufficient intelligence to benefit from a debate of reform of social programs. "Pretty soon," said Reform Party leader Preston Manning, "she won't be able to discuss the election because it's too important."*

I also look forward to continuing to work with you in my new capacity.
> Robert Rubin, *President Clinton's chief economic adviser, in 1993, in a letter to former investment-house clients. Rubin insisted the letter was not an advertisement to potential seekers of political favors.*

Politically Incorrect

I am strongly of the opinion that negroes ought to be in Africa, yellow men in Asia, and white men in Europe and America.

HARRY TRUMAN *in a letter to his wife, circa 1911. By 1940, Senator Truman, by the standards of the time and his conservative state, had become a low-key promoter of civil-rights reform, telling nearly all-white audiences in his native Missouri that "negroes have been preyed upon by all types of exploiters" and that he believed in "brotherhood of all men, not merely the brotherhood of white men, but the brotherhood of all men before the law."*

America must be kept American. Biological laws show . . . that Nordics deteriorate when mixed with other races.

Vice President CALVIN COOLIDGE in 1921, in support of national origins immigration quotas that favored immigrants from predominantly white cultures

---------------- **Reality Check** ----------------

Mr. Kremlin himself was distinguished for ignorance, for he had only one idea—and that was wrong.

BENJAMIN DISRAELI

──────────── ◆ ────────────

You are.

President GERALD FORD to Vicki Carr, a singer with Mexican ancestry, who at the end of a concert at the White House asked the president, "What's your favorite Mexican dish?"

I am delighted with some of the women that our [Republican] Senate candidates are going to be taking on because they will be easier to beat.

GEORGE BUSH in 1992, on the Senate races

A very positive message.

Vice President DAN QUAYLE in 1992, after listening to a sermon in which a Georgia minister condemned homosexuality as "satanic"

[They're] trying to prove their manhood.

Presidential candidate ROSS PEROT in 1992, describing women reporters who ask irksome questions

[They] seemed to be saying, "Here, I've got breasts. Vote for me."

Former Pennsylvania Democratic Party chairman LARRY YATCH in 1992, on the strength of female candidates

It is about a socialist, anti-family political movement that encourages women to leave their husbands, kill their children, practice witchcraft, destroy capitalism and become lesbians.

Televangelist and 1988 GOP presidential candidate PAT ROBERTSON, currently president of the Christian Coalition, in 1992, on the proposed Equal Rights Amendment

Where I come from, we have Cuomo the homo and then, in New York City, Dinkins the pinkens.

> J. PETER GRACE, *industrialist and adviser to Ronald Reagan on government efficiency, in 1992, on why he moved the head office of his W.R. Grace & Co. from New York to Florida*

He's a darkie.

> *Liberal member of Parliament* GILLES ROCHELEAU, *referring to a Parti Québécois member of the Quebec National Assembly in a speech in the House of Commons. In the 1993 federal election, Rocheleau held a news conference in his Hull-Aylmer riding to insist that his new Bloc Québécois party had more "authentic" Quebecois members of Parliament, and made his point by reading a list of Liberal members from Quebec with what he thought to be Jewish-sounding names.*

Whatever war you were in, I know it was before the Clinton fags-in-the-foxhole [proposal].

> *Virginia state senator* WARREN BARRY *in 1993, at a GOP testimonial dinner where many speakers, including Oliver North, made jokes about gays and blacks. Asked if he knew the word "fag" was offensive to gays, Barry said, "I don't know. I don't hang around with that crowd."*

Because she's a damn lesbian. I'm not going to put a lesbian in a position like that. If you want to call me a bigot, fine.

> *Senator* JESSE HELMS *in 1993, on his efforts to block the appointment of openly gay Roberta Achtenberg as assistant secretary of housing and urban development*

We have hobby, it's called "breeding,"
Welfare pay for baby feeding.
Kids need dentist? Wife need pills?
We get free, we got no bills.
We think America damn good place,
Too damn good for white man's race.
If they no like us, they can go,
Got lots of room in Mexico.

> Poem written by California state assemblyman WILLIAM J. KNIGHT
> in 1993 and distributed to fellow legislators.

Someone throws a party called Tailhook, and some lady decides a month later she's a victim, and we all pay for it in higher hotel costs.

> Newly elected GOP Representative BILL BAKER in 1994, on a
> Nevada jury decision ordering the Las Vegas Hilton to pay $6.7
> million to former Navy Lieutenant Paula Coughlin for not protecting
> her against sexual assault at the annual Tailhook Association
> convention of naval aviators

It's a hell of a challenge.

> Senator CONRAD BURNS of Montana in 1994, when asked by a
> constituent how he could live in Washington, D.C., "with all
> those niggers"

The problem with AIDS is: you got it, you die. So why are we spending money on the issue?

> DENNIS REHBERG, lieutenant governor of Montana, in 1994, on
> budget cuts to hospitals

You are articulate. You are handsome. You are young. You have the opportunity to provide a unique level of leadership.

Senator DIANNE FEINSTEIN in 1994, offering a politically incorrect endorsement at the Senate confirmation hearing for Deval Patrick, nominated to head the Justice Department's Civil Rights Division

[They] want to put homos in the military.

Representative RANDY (DUKE) CUNNINGHAM (R–Calif.) in 1995, lumping lawmakers who want to apply the law to military pollution with those who want to allow openly declared homosexuals to serve in the armed forces. Responding to criticism of the remark, Cunningham said, "It's not a bigoted statement. . . . Let me say that I used the shorthand term and should have said 'homosexuals' instead of 'homos.' We do misspeak sometimes."

We are now supportive of the Straits of Juan de Fuca, but I'm afraid the Gays of Juan de Fuca will have to take care of themselves.

PRESTON MANNING, Reform Party leader, in remarks at the 1995 Ottawa Press Gallery dinner

It's the Anglo-Saxon male that's endangered today.

HELEN CHENOWETH (R–Idaho) in 1994, in her successful campaign to become a freshman congresswoman

·12·

Invective and Ridicule

Availability was the only ability sought by the Whigs.

Senator THOMAS HART BENTON *of Missouri in 1839, on Whig presidential candidate William Henry Harrison, who became 23rd president of the United States*

——— Reality Check ———

Mr. Speaker, I withdraw. Half the Cabinet are not asses.

British statesman BENJAMIN DISRAELI, *on being asked to withdraw his comment in parliamentary debate that half the cabinet were asses*

♦

He has the backbone of a chocolate eclair.

THEODORE ROOSEVELT, *assistant secretary of the Navy, in 1897, on President William McKinley. Three years later, Roosevelt won election as vice president on a ticket headed by McKinley, and in 1901 succeeded to the presidency when McKinley was felled by an assassin's bullets.*

[**H**e has] thrown his diaper into the ring.

> *Interior Secretary* HAROLD L. ICKES *in 1939, on learning that*
> *Thomas Dewey had announced he would run against Franklin*
> *Roosevelt. Dewey, then 37, was only two years older than the*
> *constitutionally required minimum age for the presidency.*

To err is Truman.

> *Attributed to the wife of Senator Robert A. Taft (R–Ohio), in*
> *reference to Harry Truman during his first term as president*

Eisenhower doesn't know the first thing about politics.

> *President* HARRY TRUMAN *in 1950, asked by General Douglas*
> *MacArthur what he thought of the rumors that Ike was interested in a*
> *run at the presidency in 1952*

Gross terminological inexactitude.

> *Comment made in substitution for "deliberate falsification" in a 1966*
> *British parliamentary debate by a member of Parliament who was*
> *ordered by the House Speaker to withdraw his assertion of lying on the*
> *part of a fellow member. Questions in Commons debate addressed to a*
> *cabinet minister must not be "tendentious, controversial, ironic,*
> *vague, frivolous or repetitive."*

Joe, you've got a little baby boy. Well, you take his little building
blocks and go up and explain to Jerry Ford what we're trying to do.

> *President* LYNDON JOHNSON *to one of his assistants, referring to*
> *GOP House leader Gerald Ford, who opposed an LBJ public housing*
> *initiative. Ford's problem, as LBJ saw it, was that he had "played*
> *football too long without a helmet" and, as a result, was "so dumb he*
> *can't walk and fart at the same time."*

They used to be fairly inventive about the insults, but
nowadays there's an awful lot of just seeing how much they
can get away with.

> *British author* PHIL MASON, *who compiles parliamentary*
> *insults, in 1994, complaining that 19th-century slurs*
> *such as "guttersnipe" and "seditious blasphemer" have*
> *long since given way to tame modernities such as "old*
> *Etonian twerp," "hampster," and "Mr. Oil Can"*

───────────────── ◆ ─────────────────

Dole's just a hatchet man.... He's so unpopular he couldn't peddle
beer on a troopship.

> *Senator* BILL SAXBE (R–Ohio) *in 1971, on the penchant of freshman*
> *Senate colleague Bob Dole for making publicity-*
> *generating pronouncements*

[He's] a stupid bore who couldn't get a job in pictures, which is why he
went into politics.

> *Attributed to* FRANK SINATRA, *referring to Ronald Reagan, in Shirley*
> *MacLaine's 1995 autobiography. Sinatra, a friend of Nancy Reagan*
> *and master of ceremonies at one of the most lavish of President*
> *Reagan's 1981 inaugural balls, responded, "It's amazing what a broad*
> *will do for a buck."*

A triumph of the embalmer's art.

> GORE VIDAL *on Ronald Reagan's agelessness*

Shut up, you old windbag.

> *British Parliament member* WILLIE HAMILTON *to fellow member Nicholas Winterton in 1986 parliamentary debate*

Stooge.

> *Sobriquet that House Speaker* TIP O'NEILL (D–Mass.) *gave freshman congressman Newt Gingrich—as in the Three Stooges. The other stooges, for O'Neill, were Congressmen Bob Walker of Pennsylvania and Vin Webber of Minnesota.*

He looks like a lawnmower gone berserk.

> JOHN CROSBIE *in 1993, on fellow Canadian parliamentarian Herb Gray's hairstyle*

I suppose if you're Mr. Trudeau it's kind of difficult to get up in the morning and look in the mirror and know you've seen perfection for the last time all day. It's quite a burden to bear.

> *Canadian prime minister* BRIAN MULRONEY *in 1992, on former prime minister Pierre Trudeau, who opposed Mulroney's constitutional reform initiatives*

[He had] just been there—period.

> ALEXANDER HAIG *in 1988, on George Bush, upon dropping out of the race for the GOP presidential nomination and endorsing Bob Dole, who, in contrast, "had been there and made a difference"*

What's the difference between a politician and a catfish? One is a wide-mouthed, bottom-feeding slime sucker—and the other is a fish.

> *Reform Party leader* PRESTON MANNING, *campaigning for election in 1993*

What do you call 10 senators and 10 MPs at the bottom of the Rideau Canal? It's a start.

> *Reform Party leader* PRESTON MANNING, *campaigning for election in 1993*

As leader of the Progressive Conservatives I thought he put too much stress on the adjective and not enough on the noun.

> *Former British prime minister* MARGARET THATCHER *in 1993, on Canadian prime minister Brian Mulroney*

They may have changed the driver of the getaway car, but the Mulroney gang is still in the back seat.

> *Liberal Party leader* JEAN CHRÉTIEN, *campaigning in 1993, attempting to boost his own prospects with reminders of the unpopular Tory regime of recently resigned Tory prime minister Brian Mulroney*

---------------- **Reality Check** ----------------

The art of politics is learning to walk with your back to the wall, your elbows high, and a smile on your face.

> *Canadian prime minister* JEAN CHRÉTIEN, *on the need to keep the invective weapon at the ready*

----------------- ◆ -----------------

You don't seem to have enough sense for me to waste my time on, and since you don't want to hear from one of my workers, any one of which has more brains than you and all of your ancestors, I will say adios.

Texas state senator TEMPLE DICKSON *in a 1993 letter to a constituent who complained about a bill that Dickson proposed*

He is the David Duke of Canadian politics.

Canadian deputy prime minister SHEILA COPPS *on Reform Party leader Preston Manning. Duke, a Louisiana politician, is a former leader in the Ku Klux Klan.*

Warren Christopher is like Cyrus Vance—without the charisma.

Popular joke in Washington, D.C., in reference to Bill Clinton's likely nominee for secretary of state

This wouldn't have happened if Warren Christopher was alive.

Widespread Washington saying in 1993–1994, invoked to explain foreign policy setbacks at Christopher's State Department

They can kiss my rear end, if they can leap that high.

California governor PETE WILSON *in 1993, responding to Democrat critics of his proposals to reform laws dealing with illegal immigration*

Reality Check

I beseech you, in the bowels of Christ, think it possible you may be mistaken.

OLIVER CROMWELL

I have been told she does not have a grandfather or a great-grandfather who was a slave, that she came from Trinidad or Jamaica or somewhere.

> *Senator* JESSE HELMS *in 1993, on Senator Carol Moseley-Braun, the first African-American in the Senate, who had recently opposed a Helms amendment to preserve the Confederate flag*

He's got a mean little temper. Maybe he ought to go home.

> *Former Arizona senator* BARRY GOLDWATER *in 1993, on Bob Dole. Two years later Goldwater endorsed Dole's presidential bid, saying, "Bob Dole is a man whose courage and conviction have been tested again and again."*

Given the current occupant, it may be better called "The Director of Wasted Time, Going to Fancy Lunches and Not Doing Much of Anything Else."

> *A spokesperson for New York City mayor David Dinkins in 1993, on a new name for the office of New York City Council president Andrew Stein, who was expected to challenge Dinkins for the mayoralty in 1994*

Maybe we can call this his military service. Three hours is more than he had before.

> *Commander* BILL GORTNEY *of the USS Theodore Roosevelt in 1993, on Bill Clinton, during the president's tour of his aircraft carrier*

What I meant was that he has a colostomy bag the size of a walnut.
New Zealand prime minister R. D. MULDOON in a 1994
parliamentary debate, apologizing on request for his previous comment
that an opposition backbencher was guilty of "having a brain the size
of a walnut and wearing a colostomy bag"

My views of him are somewhat similar to those of a fire hydrant
toward a dog.
JIM WRIGHT in 1988, asked about his feelings toward Newt Gingrich

Whore.
Label that Representative PETE STARK (D–Calif.) applied in a 1995
committee debate to Representative Nancy Johnson (R–Conn.),
whom he accused of being a "whore" for the insurance industry—a
comment for which he later made a formal apology

The guy's a meathead.
Tory revenue minister GARTH TURNER, dismissing Liberal Party
leader Jean Chrétien's economic policies during the 1993 federal
election. Turner, who quickly withdrew his comment, was defeated a
few days later by one of Chrétien's local candidates.

You didn't need them; you kept killing them.

> *Former New York governor and capital punishment opponent* MARIO
> CUOMO *in 1995, responding to former Texas governor Ann Richards'*
> *assertion that she had built more prisons than had Cuomo, who had*
> *just claimed to have "built more prison cells than any governor in*
> *history; all the governors together didn't build as many as I did."*

Barney Fag.

> *Representative* RICHARD K. ARMEY *in 1995, referring—by a slip of*
> *the tongue, he later insisted—to Massachusetts congressman Barney*
> *Frank, who is gay. Frank dismissed Armey's assertion that he had*
> *been a victim of "trouble with alliteration," saying, "I rule out that it*
> *was an innocent mispronunciation. I turned to my own expert, my*
> *mother, who reports that in 59 years of marriage, no one ever*
> *introduced her as Elsie Fag."*

I appreciate Representative Frank trying to enhance my dull image,
but in terms of obsession with sex, I'm not in Barney's league.

> *Senator* SAM NUNN *(D–Ga.) in 1993, responding to Frank's*
> *insistence that the senator is "obsessed with sex and involved in an*
> *anti-gay witch hunt"*

You told us you would be family friendly. You forgot to tell us it would
be the Addams family.

> *Representative* BARNEY FRANK *in 1995, on the cost-cutting zealotry*
> *of his GOP adversaries in the House during the first 100 days of the*
> *104th Congress*

Some Democrats are trying very hard to be reptiles, too.

George Bushnell, *president of the American Bar Association, in 1995, apologizing after GOP lawmakers complained about a Bushnell speech in which he attacked the "reptilian bastards" who opposed funding for the federal Legal Services Corp.—a reference seen as an unflattering play on the first name of GOP House leader Newt Gingrich*

Reality Check

I don't want to see the Republican Party ride to political victory on the four horsemen of calumny—fear, ignorance, bigotry, and smear.

Senator Margaret Chase Smith (R–Maine) *in 1950, repudiating the character-assassination tactics of fellow GOP Senator Joseph McCarthy*

---◆---

If he wants to get into veterinarian metaphors he should have been spayed, fixed when he was a young man and maybe he'd get a second term as president.

Representative Robert Dornan (R–Calif.) *in 1995, after President Clinton said that Dornan needs an anti-rabies shot. Dornan had accused Clinton of giving "aid and comfort to the enemy" during the Vietnam War, labeled Clinton a "draft-dodging adulterer" and called him "a sleazeball who can't keep his pants on."*

Last year I was Bambi, this year Stalin. From Disneyland to dictatorship in 12 short months.

British Labor Party leader TONY BLAIR *in 1995, on the name-calling tactics of Prime Minister John Major's Tories*

If hypocrisy were an Olympic event, Al would win the gold, silver and bronze.

MARK GREEN, *unsuccessful Democratic opponent of Al D'Amato in a race for a New York seat in the U.S. Senate, in 1995, responding to D'Amato's attacks on Green in his newly published autobiography*

·13·

Media Relations

Beat the Press

Reality Check

I deplore . . . the putrid state into which the newspapers
have passed, and the malignity, the vulgarity and
mendacious spirit of those who write them. . . . These
ordures are rapidly depraving the public taste.

THOMAS JEFFERSON

♦

Why the deuce is it that they have such an itching for abusing me?
President MARTIN VAN BUREN, *on being attacked in the newspapers*

Now remember, don't quote me.
President CALVIN COOLIDGE *in 1924, after answering a simple "no"
to each question put to him by reporters at a campaign appearance*

199

I know every one of these 50 fellows. There isn't one of them has enough sense to pound sand into a rat hole.

President HARRY TRUMAN *in 1948, campaigning for reelection, on learning of a* Newsweek *poll of 50 highly regarded political writers, 50 of whom predicted Truman would lose the election*

——————— Reality Check ———————

I have pretty much made up my mind to run for President. . . . I am going to own up in advance to all the wickedness I have done, and if any Congressional committee is disposed to prowl around my biography in the hope of discovering any dark and deadly deed that I have secreted, why—let it prowl.

I candidly acknowledge that I ran away at the Battle of Gettysburg. . . . I want my country saved, but I preferred to have somebody else save it. I entertain that preference yet. . . . The rumor that I buried a dead aunt under my grapevine was correct. The vine needed fertilizing, my aunt had to be buried, and I dedicated her to this high purpose. Does that unfit me for the Presidency? The Constitution of our country does not say so. . . . I admit also that I am not a friend of the poor man. I regard the poor man, in his present condition, as so much wasted raw material. Cut up and properly canned, he might be made useful to fatten the natives of the cannibal islands and to improve our export trade with that region.

MARK TWAIN *in an 1897 column in the* New York Evening Post, *confronting the character issue*

——————————— ◆ ———————————

Television is to news what bumper stickers are to philosophy.

RICHARD NIXON

I'll be glad to reply to or dodge your questions, depending on what I think will help our election most.

GEORGE BUSH *in 1980, campaigning in South Carolina*

It's been such a long journey, so many 24-hour days, and there are so many times I'd see you scrambling for a bus in the darkness or shivering in your parkas on a tarmac somewhere at dawn, and I'd think: That's tough. Too bad. It's not my problem. Get a job. Get a haircut.

GEORGE BUSH's *farewell comments in 1988 to reporters on his press plane a few days before the end of the 1988 presidential campaign*

That's a good question. Let me try to evade you.

Former presidential candidate PAUL TSONGAS *in 1992, when asked if he was more interested in promoting his own policies than helping Democratic nominee Bill Clinton*

I feel like I've been raped by you guys already, okay, and I just figure this rape has gone on long enough. Quite frankly, for me to continue to lay back and let you guys do this is just asinine.

Democratic Senate candidate CAROL MOSELEY-BRAUN *of Illinois in 1992, to reporters asking her about alleged ethical lapses that included nondisclosure of a $29,000 gift from her mother and evidence that as Cook County recorder of deeds she placed city funds in the non-interest-bearing account of a political associate*

Avoid this crowd like the plague. And if they quote you, make damn sure they heard you.

> BARBARA BUSH *in 1992, in advice to Hillary Clinton on the media surrounding them during a tour of the White House. Mrs. Clinton's reply: "That's right. I know that feeling already."*

Special note to all press from the highest authority: Don't touch the cat again.

> *Written statement from* BILL CLINTON *in 1992, to photographers who used catnip to lure First Pet-elect Socks into camera range*

Thank you, Lord, for a free press.... But gracious Father, investigative reporting seems epidemic in an election year—its primary objective to defame political candidates. Seeking their own reputation, they destroy another's as they search relentlessly, microscopically for some ancient skeleton in a person's life. Eternal God, help these self-appointed "vacuum cleaner journalists" to discover how unproductive and divisive their efforts are.

> RICHARD C. HALVERSON, *Senate chaplain, in 1992, in a prayer given on the Senate floor*

If he starts sleeping through cabinet meetings, you'll know the transformation is complete.

> *Former Bush press secretary* MARLIN FITZWATER *in 1993, on ex-Reagan adviser David Gergen's mission to reshape Bill Clinton's image*

That's the president of the United States you're talking about, pinhead.

Vice President AL GORE *to talk-show host David Letterman, who had joked that Bill Clinton loves to hear the words, "Would you like fries with that?"*

Like I can't go on their TV network unless I look good.

Attorney General JANET RENO *in 1993, on network demands that she wear makeup on air*

I have fought more damn battles here for more things than any president has in 20 years with the possible exception of Reagan's first budget and not gotten one damn bit of credit from the knee-jerk liberal press. I am sick and tired of it, and you can put that in the damn article.

President BILL CLINTON *in 1993, in parting comments to* Rolling Stone *interviewers visiting the White House.* Rolling Stone *heartily endorsed Clinton's presidential bid in 1992.*

Raising the blood pressure of reporters and editors like you so easily and so often.

Senator JESSE HELMS *in 1994, when asked by a reporter what he considered to be his most impressive accomplishment*

I'd be ashamed to make my living the way you make yours, asshole.

JAKE GARN, former Utah senator, in a 1994 confrontation with reporter Steve Wilson during a corporate-funded ski event. Wilson's reply, according to Garn: "It's better than being a bought-and-paid-for U.S. senator."

You want happy quotes or hate quotes?

DAVID TELL, communications director at William Kristol's right-wing think tank, the Project for the Republican Future, when a reporter called asking for Kristol's view on his role in helping engineer the GOP's successful strategy in taking control of the Senate and the House in 1994

You will never be their friends. They don't want to be your friends. Some female reporter will come up to one of you and start batting her eyes and ask you to go to lunch. And you'll think, "Wow, I'm only a freshman. Cokie Roberts wants to take me to lunch. I've really made it!" Don't fall for this. This is not the time to get moderate. This is not the time to start trying to be liked.

Political commentator RUSH LIMBAUGH in 1994, addressing the freshman class of GOP members of Congress, who made him an honorary member of their caucus

From Vietnam and Watergate, the press is in a long cycle in which scandal-mongering and personal attacks have replaced policy debate.

NEWT GINGRICH in 1994, on perceived distortions of his views. When a reporter asked if Gingrich's own pit-bull style of rhetoric contributed to this cycle, Gingrich responded, "Isn't it a fact that you bear some responsibility, too? Isn't it? Answer me. Yes or no?"

Reformers are now avoiding jokes that might reflect insensitively on personal disabilities or personal beliefs, like the one about the dyslexic, agnostic insomniac who lay awake nights wondering whether there is a Dog.

I will repeat that again a little more slowly, since there are people here tonight from the *Calgary Herald* editorial board. It's a reference to a joke about the dyslexic, agnostic insomniac who lay awake nights wondering whether there is a Dog.

PRESTON MANNING, *leader of Canada's Reform Party, at the 1995 Ottawa Press Gallery dinner*

Look, half the time when I see the evening news, I wouldn't be for me, either.

BILL CLINTON *in 1995, on a precampaign swing through Montana and Colorado*

You can write it up any f——g way you want.

Representative ROBERT DORNAN (R–Calif.)*, presidential candidate, in 1995, when* Newsweek *asked him about an apparent contradiction between his boast of being "a s—t-hot fighter pilot" who graduated at the top of his 1955 flight-school class, and a career record that consisted of having cracked up three jets and a helicopter in a less-than-a-year-long stint in active duty and the Reserves*

Shouts from the Peanut Gallery

The heads of conservatives have a puny and deficient look, a certain callowness and concavity, as if they were prematurely exposed on one or both sides, or were made to lie or pack together, as when several nuts are formed under the same burr where only one should have been. We wonder to see such a head wear a whole hat. Such as these naturally herd together for mutual protection.

HENRY DAVID THOREAU *in 1848*

The craftiest and most dishonest politician that ever disgraced an office in America.

The Illinois State Register *on President Abraham Lincoln, an Illinois native son*

Nero fiddled while Rome burned, but Coolidge only snores.

H. L. MENCKEN *on the avowedly do-nothing administration of President Calvin Coolidge*

If they confess that there is the slightest chance that Mr. Roosevelt may die or become incapacitated in the next four years, they are faced with the grinning skeleton of Truman the bankrupt, Truman the pliant tool of Boss Pendergast in looting Kansas City's county government. Truman the yes-man and apologist in the Senate for political gangsters.

The Chicago Tribune's *editorial board greets newly elected vice president Harry Truman with an assessment whose even-handedness would mark its later regard of him as President Truman*

I haven't checked these figures but 87 years ago, I think it was, a number of individuals organized a government setup here in this country, I believe it covered certain eastern areas, with this idea they were following up, based on a sort of national independence arrangement. . . . We have to make up our minds right here and now, as I see it, they didn't put out all that blood, perspiration and—well, that they didn't just make a dry run here, that all of us, under God, that is, the God of our choice, shall beef up this idea about freedom and liberty and those kind of arrangements, and that government of all individuals, by all individuals and for the individuals shall not pass out of the world picture.

> *A reporter's parody of President Dwight Eisenhower's likely rendition of the Gettysburg Address*

---------------- **Reality Check** ----------------

Journalism is the last refuge of the vaguely talented.

> WALTER LIPPMANN

---------------- ♦ ----------------

I believe there really is a "new Nixon," a maturer and mellower man who is no longer clawing his way to the top.

> WALTER LIPPMANN *in 1968, on Richard Nixon*

[President Nixon is] the greatest moral leader of the last third of this century.

> JOHN MCLAUGHLIN, *Jesuit priest and Nixon confessor turned talk-show host (PBS's "The McLaughlin Group"), in 1974, speaking from the White House steps at the invitation of Nixon aides shortly before the president's resignation over the Watergate affair*

Clinton's background—Yale Law, Rhodes scholar, a lawyer wife who used her maiden name and had her own successful career—helped bring him to the notice of the national media when he first took office (some, absurdly, mentioned this 32-year-old incoming governor of a small state as a possible president).

> The Almanac of American Politics, *1984 edition*

The Democrats are the party of government activism, the party that says government can make you richer, smarter, taller, and get the chickweed out of your lawn. Republicans are the party that says government doesn't work, and then get elected and prove it.

P. J. O'ROURKE *in* Parliament of Whores *(1991)*

Reality Check

What the mob thirsts for is not good government in itself, but the merry chase of a definite exponent of bad government.

H. L. MENCKEN *in 1914*

Excuse me, George Herbert, irregular-heart-beating, read-my-lying-lipping, slipping-in-the-polls, do-nothing, deficit-raising, make-less-money-than-Millie-the-White-House-dog-last-year, Quayle-loving, sushi-puking Bush! I don't remember inviting your ass on my show!

ARSENIO HALL *in 1992, responding to an announcement that President Bush was considering appearances on talk shows with the exception of "The Arsenio Hall Show"*

It's true Clinton didn't serve in Vietnam, but during his marriage he's been listed several times as missing in action.

Talk-show host DAVID LETTERMAN *in 1992*

Absent a scandal or economic collapse, Clinton's a goner.

Pundit FRED BARNES *in* The New Republic *in May 1992, declaring Bill Clinton's presidential candidacy D.O.A.*

[He's just another] well-wired, pork-producing, inside-the-
Beltway operator.

Political columnist GEORGE WILL *on Newt Gingrich, who began
promoting himself as someone who could deliver to his constituents in
Cobb County, Georgia, after coming close to being defeated in 1992.
Will concluded that, his calls for term limits notwithstanding, Capitol
Hill veteran Gingrich is "a case study of the primacy of careerism in
the life of the modern Congressman."*

―――――――― **Reality Check** ――――――――

At the end of the Reagan era all the presidential
candidates looked like local TV news guys . . . Stepford
candidates with prefab epiphanies, inauthentic men for an
inauthentic age.

PEGGY NOONAN, *speechwriter in the Reagan and Bush
administrations, in* What I Saw At The Revolution

――――――――――◆――――――――――

He ate everything but the drapes. . . . He's a man who does like to put
it down.

TOM BROKAW *in 1993, on Bill Clinton's luncheon with TV network
news anchors*

Even a lecher deserves to be undisturbed in his constitutional rights.

*A Boston Globe editorial in 1993, defending Senator Bob
Packwood's right to keep his diaries private*

Did you know there's a White House dog?

> RUSH LIMBAUGH *in 1993, referring first to White House cat Socks,*
> *and then holding up a photograph of 13-year-old Chelsea Clinton,*
> *daughter of President Clinton*

Are you saying the president should *kill* Rush Limbaugh? He could have a heart attack and die.

> DEE DEE MYERS, *White House press secretary, in 1993, on whether*
> *Bill Clinton should consider taming the 300-pound conservative talk-*
> *show host by jogging with him*

The reporter used to gain status by dining with his subjects; now he gains status by dining out on them.

ADAM GOPNIK, New Yorker *correspondent, in 1995*

[**S**he] was born needing her face ironed.

RUSH LIMBAUGH *in 1994, on Texas governor Ann Richards*

He's turned the corner, mastered the job, bridged the
stature gap. Until next week.

> Newsweek's *"Conventional Wisdom Watch"* in 1993,
> on President Clinton's success in securing passage of the
> North American Free Trade Agreement

———— ♦ ————

[**W**ho] is "the loneliest monk"?

> TABITHA SOREN, *reporter for MTV, in 1993, after she interviewed
> Bill Clinton, who said he once dreamed of playing sax with jazz great
> Thelonius Monk*

JOYCELYN ELDERS: NAZISM REBORN

> *Headline in a 1993 edition of the newsletter* Clintonwatch, *published
> by the right-wing group Citizens United, in which CU president Floyd
> Brown takes issue with Elders's strong language. "The President's pick
> for Surgeon General attracts attention not only for her stridently liberal
> positions but also for her unusually blunt manner of expressing them."*

———— **Reality Check** ————

The most distinctive thing to emerge in the American
media recently has been not cynicism at all but a kind of
weird, free-form nastiness—spleen without purpose,
grayness with an attitude.

> ADAM GOPNIK, New Yorker *correspondent, in 1994*

———— ♦ ————

There are some people, like Senator Alfonse D'Amato, he comes on . . . and he rants and yells and screams and calls you every name in the book. And then during the break he leans over and sort of goes like this, and says, "How am I doing? Is that what you want?"

MICHAEL KINSLEY, co-host of CNN's Crossfire, on how certain guests perform for the camera

Kathleen Gingrich: The only thing [Newt] ever told me is that [Bill Clinton is] smart. That he's an intelligent man. That he's not very practical, but he's intelligent. I can't tell you what he said about Hillary.

Connie Chung: You can't?

Mrs. Gingrich: I can't.

Ms. Chung: Why don't you just whisper it to me, just between you and me?

Mrs. Gingrich: "She's a bitch." About the only thing he ever said about her. I think they had some meeting, you know, and she takes over . . . but with Newty there, she can't.

Exchange between KATHLEEN GINGRICH, mother of Newt Gingrich, and the host of the CBS news program Eye to Eye With Connie Chung, the transcript of which was released on January 5, 1995, the day Gingrich was sworn in as House Speaker

When Pat Buchanan announced his candidacy, some people . . . ran onto the stage carrying signs that read, "Pat Buchanan is a racist." And those were his *supporters*.

> *Late-night TV comic* CONAN O'BRIEN *at the 1995 White House Correspondents' Association annual dinner, where large parts of his routine bombed. When it was his turn to speak, President Clinton looked over at O'Brien and said, "I feel your pain."*

I admit it—the liberal media were never that powerful, and the whole thing was often used as an excuse by conservatives for conservative failures.

WILLIAM KRISTOL, *former adviser to Vice President Dan Quayle and founding publisher and editor of* The Standard, *in 1995*

◆

I don't feel that I am fueling the lunatic fringe.

G. GORDON LIDDY, *convicted Watergate burglar and right-wing talk-show host, in 1995. On his show, Liddy had talked about his new hobby of using figures labeled "Bill" and "Hillary" for target practice. He did apologize for advising listeners on how to retaliate against government persecution by shooting at agents of the federal Bureau of Alcohol, Tobacco and Firearms: "I take back what I said about shooting the agent in the head," Liddy said. "You should aim for the chest and the groin."*

Marty, Jean's out of control. Shred her!

Failed senatorial candidate OLIVER NORTH *in 1995, instructing an assistant to hang up on an angry caller on the first day of his new radio talk show.*

I don't have time to talk to anyone who has time to call a radio program.

Former governor ANN RICHARDS *of Texas, in 1995, on why she is bucking the trend of politicians recently ejected from office to take up new careers as talk-show hosts*

·14·

Take This Job and Shove It

This will be the commencement of the decline of my reputation.

GEORGE WASHINGTON *in 1775, on learning that the Continental Congress had voted unanimously for Washington as its choice as commander-in-chief of Continental military forces*

I have accepted a seat in the House of Representatives, and thereby have consented to my own ruin, to your ruin, and to the ruin of our children. I give you this warning that you may prepare your mind for your fate.

JOHN ADAMS, *second president of the United States*

I have no ambition to govern men; it is a painful and thankless office.

THOMAS JEFFERSON, *third president of the United States*

Splendid misery.

THOMAS JEFFERSON, *on the presidency*

217

Politics is not the art of the possible. It consists in choosing between the disastrous and the unpalatable.

JOHN KENNETH GALBRAITH

——————————— ♦ ———————————

There is no gratitude to be expected from the public. I have found that out years ago.

JOHN A. MACDONALD, *first Canadian prime minister*

My God! What is there in this place that a man should ever want to get into it?

President JAMES A. GARFIELD, *on the presidency and the crush of office-seekers bidding for presidential favors*

Well, do you want me to appoint another horse thief for you?

President GROVER CLEVELAND, *to a party operative seeking favors for a friend*

I am in jail, and I can't get out. I've got to stay.

President WARREN HARDING, *on the presidential life*

It is hell! No other word can describe it.

WARREN HARDING, *on the presidency*

It sure is hell to be president.
President HARRY TRUMAN, *during his first year in the White House*

The people can never understand why the President does not use his supposedly great power to make 'em behave. Well, all the President is, is a glorified public relations man who spends his time flattering, kissing and kicking people to get them to do what they are supposed to do anyway.
President HARRY TRUMAN *in a 1947 letter to his sister. Truman liked to say that public life in Washington could boast more prima donnas per square foot than all the opera companies in the world.*

———————— **Reality Check** ————————

The depositary of power is always unpopular.
BENJAMIN DISRAELI

———————— ◆ ————————

Life is unfair.
President JOHN KENNEDY, *after an early setback in office*

No, she probably apologizes.
President JIMMY CARTER, *asked if his daughter Amy ever bragged to schoolmates that her father was president*

Tell me another profession where you are forgotten so quickly if the tide turns against you.
Canadian parliamentarian JOHN CROSBIE, *on politics as a career*

If I win, I win. And if I lose, I spare myself untold agony.
JOHN CROSBIE *in 1983, contemplating a run at the leadership of Canada's Progressive Conservative Party*

Why would anybody want to run for president of the United States?
GARY HART *in 1987, campaigning for the presidency, to a cousin during a visit to his hometown of Ottawa, Kansas*

Now if you have a cut, a weakness, they go after it, beat on it, try to exploit it until they kill you.
Representative JIM WRIGHT (D–Tex.) *in 1987, on the shark-infested waters of Washington political life*

Don't count on it, Father. That's not the way it appears to me, man.
GEORGE BUSH *in 1992, after a priest said the president has "a lot of power and a lot of clout"*

There are always going to be people who want to be president, and some days I'd like to give it to them.
President BILL CLINTON *in 1993*

Senators are expected to shave and wear socks.

> *Author and former state legislator* JOHN GRISHAM *in 1993, on his*
> *decision not to seek a Senate seat*

———— Reality Check ————

Have y'ever wondered why in Ameriky they build th'
triumphal arches out a'brick? 'Tis so they'll have some'thin'
handy t'throw at th' conquerin' hero when he passes thr'.

> FINLEY PETER DUNNE

———————— ♦ ————————

I came here as prime steak and now I feel like low-grade hamburger.

> JOYCELYN ELDERS, *recently confirmed as surgeon general, in 1993,*
> *on her view of politics in Washington compared to life back home*
> *in Arkansas*

One expects Tories to buy into "great man" theories of history, but not
social democrats. Conservatives choose a leader, follow him until he
drops, then eat him alive.

> TONY PENIKETT, *leader of the New Democratic Party in the Yukon*
> *Territory, in 1994*

You just work like a dog, do well, the test scores are up, the kids are looking better, the dropout rate is down, and all of a sudden you've got some jerk who's running for public office telling everybody it's a sham and it isn't real.

> Governor ANN RICHARDS (D–Tex.) in 1994, saying her GOP
> opponent, George W. Bush, is too negative about conditions in
> the state

———————— **Reality Check** ————————

What this White House really needs is a chief of staff who can read Machiavelli in the original Italian.

> MACK McLARTY, recently resigned as chief of staff to
> President Bill Clinton, in 1994. McLarty's nickname
> among Clinton staffers was "Mack the Nice."

———————————— ◆ ————————————

I don't suppose there's any public figure that's ever been subject to any more violent personal attacks than I have. . . . And that's fine. I deal with them. But I don't believe it's the work of God.

> BILL CLINTON in 1994, in a talk-show appearance in which he
> criticized the religious right for making "scurrilous" charges against him
> and blamed the media for encouraging "cynicism" among Americans

Reality Check

Democracy is the process by which people choose the man who'll get the blame.

BERTRAND RUSSELL

◆

It's like learning to play the violin in public.

BOB RAE *in 1994, on the frustrations that followed after he became premier of Ontario*

A guy with Peaceable Texans for Guns called me the other day to say he was going to kill me.

Texas state representative KEITH OAKLEY *in 1995. Oakley had proposed a state referendum on whether to allow citizens to carry concealed weapons.*

I've always been a big supporter of the Constitutional right of the people to peaceably assemble and petition government for redress of grievances. It's just that I never envisioned it taking the form of thousands of people screaming "You asshole" at me.

Former U.S. senator and Connecticut governor LOWELL WEICKER *in 1994, on the joys of retiring from public life*

It's tiring and stressful. It's not just the hours. It's having to think while you're here.

Representative HENRY HYDE *in 1995, on the exhausting work required to pass elements of the GOP's "Contract With America" in the first 100 days of the 104th Congress*

──────── ◆ ────────

·15·

Explications

To be a statesman you must first get elected.

> J. WILLIAM FULBRIGHT, *Arkansas senator whose enlightened internationalism contrasted with his consistent opposition to civil-rights bills*

I am not a crook. I've earned every penny I've got.

> RICHARD NIXON *in 1973*

The historical record is that 19 years ago, I used marijuana once at a party... in New Orleans.... It didn't have any effect on me. As a matter of fact, I never went back and revisited it.

> NEWT GINGRICH *in 1987*

Bugs drawn to the light.

> *Reform Party leader* PRESTON MANNING *in 1993, explaining the attraction his party seems to hold for conservative extremists*

Reality Check

We conferred endlessly and futilely, and arrived at the place from which we started. Then we did what we knew we had to do in the first place, and we failed as we knew we would.

WINSTON CHURCHILL

It's just very hard to have a personal relationship. It probably attracts those who in part get their ego needs from a larger audience because they're too frightened to get it from a smaller audience.

NEWT GINGRICH, *asked about the role that politics played in his failed first marriage*

My recollection is a little different. What passes between two people . . . It's just very difficult, very painful.

NEWT GINGRICH *in 1989, responding to allegations of his having gone to his wife's hospital room carrying divorce papers while she was recovering from cancer surgery*

———————— Reality Check ————————

Even politicians are human.

Canadian prime minister PIERRE TRUDEAU

——————— ♦ ———————

Unlike the president, I inhaled. And then I threw up.

CHRISTINE TODD WHITMAN, *governor-elect of New Jersey, in 1993, on the difference between her history with marijuana and that of Bill Clinton*

I'm no Hillary Clinton.

> *Senator* ALFONSE D'AMATO *in 1994, defending his one-day,*
> *$37,000 profit from trading in commodities, an amount a little shy of*
> *the $100,000 that Mrs. Clinton made during a period of several*
> *months of late-1970s commodities trading*

As a 26-year-old Ph.D. in economics, I could have quit my job at [Texas] A&M and joined the Army. I would have probably ended up working in some library somewhere or maybe teaching at West Point or working in the Pentagon. But I thought what I was doing at Texas A&M was important.

> *Senator* PHIL GRAMM, *defending the deferments he received from*
> *serving in Vietnam. His own draft avoidance didn't stop Gramm from*
> *campaigning against Texas Democratic politician Chet Edwards in*
> *1990 with the accusation that Edwards wasn't fit for public office*
> *because he "didn't serve in the military."*

That was a sign we were alive and were in graduate school in that era.

> NEWT GINGRICH *in 1994, on his admission that he had once smoked*
> *marijuana. The topic was raised as a counterpoint to Gingrich's 1994*
> *attack on the "counterculture" Clinton White House.*

In the 1970s, things happened—period. That's the most I'll ever say. . . . I start with the assumption that all human beings sin and that all human beings are in fact human . . . so all I'll say is that I've led a human life.

> NEWT GINGRICH *in 1994, on allegations that he was not faithful to*
> *his first wife*

Critics are attempting to use a brother-in-law investment in a movie that was never made to tie me to the people I don't know and things that I have no knowledge of.

Senator PHIL GRAMM *in 1995, on a report in* The New Republic *that a blind $7,500 investment he made 20 years ago turned into a proposal for an R-rated movie to be called* Beauty Queens *and to be directed by Mark Lester, director of* Tricia's Wedding, *a soft-porn spoof of the wedding of President Nixon's daughter Tricia*

———————— **Reality Check** ————————

If hypocrisy were gold, the Capitol would be Fort Knox.
Senator JOHN MCCAIN *(R–Ariz.) in 1994*

———————————— ♦ ————————————

As Speaker, who is a Ph.D. in history, I think I have the right to select an academic who has legitimate credentials and who I believe has the enthusiasm and the belief in the American process to help a generation of young people learn why America works the way it does. And I think I may be peculiarly, of all the people who have been Speaker, in a legitimate position to make a selection that I think will be helpful in re-establishing the legitimacy of history.

NEWT GINGRICH *in 1995, on his controversial decision to fire the official historian of the House of Representatives and appoint in his stead Christina Jeffrey, a friend and fellow faculty member from Gingrich's days at Kennesaw State University, who said her new $85,000-a-year job would entail "chronicling the Speaker and doing for the Republicans what academics did for FDR." One day after rising to the defense of his appointee, Gingrich forced Jeffrey's* *resignation after learning that she had once helped to deny federal financing of an educational program about the Holocaust on the basis that it did not present the views of the Nazis and the Ku Klux Klan.*

—————— Reality Check ——————

I'm not quite there yet, I'm trying. But it's hard. I mean it's, you know, I've been a backbencher. And I mean, shucks, people didn't used to listen to even my good stuff.

NEWT GINGRICH *in 1995, on the advice of his wife, Marianne, to "go slow down, and be responsible" in what he says*

◆

·16·

Post Partum

There's nothing left but to get drunk.
> President FRANKLIN PIERCE in 1856, having been denied
> renomination for the presidency by his own party, when asked what a
> president should do after leaving office

I have one consolation. No one candidate was ever elected ex-
president by such a large majority.
> WILLIAM HOWARD TAFT in 1912, on receiving the fewest votes of
> the three presidential candidates—himself, Theodore Roosevelt, and
> the victor, Woodrow Wilson

If I'm alive, what am I doing here? And if I'm dead, why do I have to
go to the bathroom?
> THOMAS DEWEY, GOP nominee for the presidency, in 1948, saying
> that his startling defeat by Harry Truman made him feel as though he
> were in a coffin with a lily in his hand

Here's something else for the library. These are the leftovers from the president's lunch today.

> BILL MOYERS, *press secretary to President Lyndon Johnson, to Johnson's personal secretary after she had reprimanded him for continuing to dump material into his wastebasket despite a recent White House order that all memorabilia was henceforth to be saved for a planned Lyndon Johnson library*

No, the part that starts, "I do solemnly swear . . ."

> RICHARD NIXON, *soon after John Kennedy's inauguration. Nixon told JFK speechwriter Ted Sorenson that he wished he had said some of the things in JFK's inaugural address, and Sorenson then asked, "That part about, 'Ask not what your country can do for you . . .'?"*

Sock it to me?

> RICHARD NIXON *in a mid-1960s appearance on* "Rowan and Martin's Laugh-In"

Stuart E. Eizenstat occupied the most prominent position a practicing American Jew has held in American government in modern times, as the chief domestic policy adviser to President Carter from 1977 to 1981. His position has been compared by some to that held by Joseph in Egypt.

> *From* EIZENSTAT's *curriculum vitae, circa 1984*

Don't let him make any major decisions until he is entirely well. You don't make good decisions when you're sick. I was recovering from pneumonia when I made the decision not to burn the tapes.

Attributed to RICHARD NIXON *by presidential aide Lyn Nofziger as advice he received from Nixon soon after the unsuccessful assassination attempt on President Ronald Reagan in 1981*

Politics is just like show business. You have a hell of an opening, you coast for awhile, you have a hell of a closing.

RONALD REAGAN

———————— **Reality Check** ————————

How can a president not be an actor?
RONALD REAGAN, *when asked, "How could an actor become president?"*

———————— ♦ ————————

You know you're out of power when your limousine is yellow and your driver speaks Farsi.

JAMES BAKER, *secretary of state in the Bush administration, in 1993*

I'm looking for a model. I want a pair of ruby-red lips right on my ass.
Retired U.S. senator BARRY GOLDWATER *in 1993, when asked by late-night talk-show host Jay Leno if he would want a tattoo like fellow Tonight show guest Roseanne Arnold*

[Chrétien] always insisted on having good advisers around him. He knew his limitations, which is more than I can say for the rest of us.

Former prime minister PIERRE TRUDEAU *in 1993, one week after Jean Chrétien was sworn in as Canada's 20th prime minister, offering faint praise to his protege while launching a promotional tour for his memoirs*

I suppose it would be a little more interesting than an Ed McMahon museum.

Indianapolis editor HARRISON ULLMAN *in 1993, on Huntington, Indiana's, new Dan Quayle Center and Museum*

I was signing books and a very nice-looking young lady came by and said, "Mr. President, if you're still lusting in your heart, I'm available." The whole crowd broke out laughing. I blushed.

Former president JIMMY CARTER *in 1993*

Reality Check

When a man fell into his anecdotage, it was a sign for him to retire from the world.

BENJAMIN DISRAELI

◆

By leading abroad as he has done so effectively at home, President Clinton will establish himself as the world's pre-eminent statesman.

RICHARD NIXON *in 1993, endorsing Bill Clinton the foreign-policy president in a* New York Times *op-ed piece*

Quite often . . . these little guys, who might be making atomic weapons or who might be guilty of some human-rights violations or whatever, are looking for someone to listen to their problems and help them communicate.

Jimmy Carter in 1994, on observations he had while negotiating recently with dictators in North Korea, Haiti, and other hot spots

Well, for me, that would be a 72% reduction.

Senate majority leader George Mitchell in 1994, announcing his decision not to seek reelection and recalling a warning he had received from a baseball club owner that if he were to accept the post of baseball commissioner he would have to deal with "28 owners with big egos"

Reality Check

You may not know my work, but I've seen all your movies.

Former Soviet leader Mikhail Gorbachev in 1994, introducing himself to Paul Newman in a Los Angeles hotel lobby

---◆---

First, I was Millie's co-owner. Then it was Barbara's husband, the author of the best-selling book. And now it's the father of the governor-elect of Texas. And then I have to share Dana Carvey. Not going to do it. Wouldn't be prudent. Not going to do it.

Former president George Bush in 1994, speaking at the groundbreaking of the George Bush Presidential Library at Texas A&M University

It's the death of a monarchy. You could imagine Edwards with rouged cheeks and purple cape passing out doubloons to the serfs. He was the king.

> Mark McKinnon *in 1994, after four-term Louisiana governor Edwin Edwards said he would not seek reelection*

It was very worth it.

> *Representative* Michael Huffington (R–Calif.) *in 1994, after spending $28 million of his own money in a failed bid to unseat Dianne Feinstein in the U.S. Senate race*

Reality Check

It would be hard to go from a life of state dinners and exotic travels to doing Republican Lincoln Day Dinners at Nelson's Golden Glo Port-a-Pit hall in Wakarusa.

> *Political commentator* Brian Howey *in 1995, on the slim possibility of Dan Quayle running for Indiana governor. Quayle announced in February that he would not, after all, make a gubernatorial bid.*

I'm a slimeball in it, but at least it's not a big part.

> Henry Kissinger, *former secretary of state, in 1995, on how his character is portrayed in Oliver Stone's new movie,* Nixon

Well, for one thing, I find that I no longer win every golf game I play.

GEORGE BUSH *in 1994, on life after the presidency*

—————— ♦ ——————

My squinty little eyes and mastodonic nose.

Former vice president SPIRO AGNEW *in 1995, congratulating sculptor William Behrends for capturing an accurate likeness in his bust of Agnew, on the occasion of its formal unveiling in the gallery of vice-presidential busts on Capitol Hill*

Index to Quoted Sources